The rise of the Nazis

How and why did the Nazis seize power in Germany? Despite the passing of sixty years or more, the question remains heated and important discoveries continue to challenge long-standing assumptions. In *The rise of the Nazis* Conan Fischer takes stock of the current debate and concludes that certain orthodoxies require rethinking.

The book begins with an overview of the historical context within which Nazism grew, looking at the foreign relations, politics and society of Weimar and particularly at the role of the elites in the rise of Nazism. It proceeds to examine the anatomy of Nazism itself. What lent its ideology coherence and credibility? What distinguished the Nazis' programme from their competitors' and how did they project it so effectively? How was Hitler able to put together and fund an organisation so quickly and successfully that it could launch a sustained assault on Weimar? Who supported the Nazis and what were their motives? Where, precisely, does Nazism belong in the history of Europe?

In concise, readable chapters, followed by a documentary appendix, this new textbook provides the student and general reader of twentieth-century German history with an essential up-dated revision of these complex and traumatic issues.

NEW FRONTIERS IN HISTORY

series editors

Mark Greengrass
Department of History, Sheffield University

John Stevenson
Worcester College, Oxford

This important new series reflects the substantial expansion that has occurred in the scope of history syllabuses. As new subject areas have emerged and syllabuses have come to focus more upon methods of historical enquiry and knowledge of source materials, a growing need has arisen for correspondingly broad-ranging textbooks.

New Frontiers in History provides up-to-date overviews of key topics in British, European and world history, together with accompanying source material and appendices. Authors focus upon subjects where revisionist work is being undertaken, providing a fresh viewpoint which will be welcomed by students and sixth-formers. The series also explores established topics which have attracted much conflicting analysis and require a synthesis of the state of the debate.

Published titles

C. J. Bartlett Defence and diplomacy: Britain and the Great Powers, 1815–1914

Jeremy Black The politics of Britain, 1688–1800

David Brooks The age of upheaval: Edwardian politics, 1899–1914

Keith Laybourn The General Strike of 1926

Panikos Panayi Immigration, ethnicity and racism in Britain, 1815–1945

Daniel Szechi The Jacobites: Britain and Europe, 1688–1788

Forthcoming titles

Paul Bookbinder The Weimer Republic

Joanna Bourke Production and reproduction: working women in Britain, 1860–1960

Michael Braddick The nerves of state: taxation and the financing of the English state, 1558–1714

Ciaran Brady The unplanned conquest: social changes and political conflict in sixteenth-century Ireland

David Carlton Churchill and the Soviets

Carl Chinn Poverty and the urban poor in the nineteenth century

Barry Coward The Cromwellian Protectorate

Neville Kirk The rise of Labour, 1850–1920

Tony Kushner The Holocaust and its aftermath

Alan O'Day Irish Home Rule

John Whittam Fascist Italy

The rise of
the Nazis

Conan Fischer

Manchester University Press

Manchester and New York

Distributed exclusively in the USA and Canada by St. Martin's Press

Published by Manchester University Press
Oxford Road, Manchester M13 9NR, UK
and Room 400, 175 Fifth Avenue, New York, NY 10010, USA

Distributed exclusively in the USA and Canada
by St. Martin's Press, Inc., 175 Fifth Avenue, New York,
NY 10010, USA

British Library Cataloguing-in-Publication Data
A catalogue record for this book is available from the British Library

Library of Congress Cataloging-in-Publication Data
Fischer, Conan.
      The rise of the Nazis / Conan Fischer.
         p.   cm. — (New frontiers in history)
      Includes bibliographical references and index.
      ISBN 0-7190-3502-3. — ISBN 0-7190-3503-1 (pbk.)
      1. National socialism—Germany. 2. Germany—Politics and
government—1918–1933. 3. Electioneering—Germany—History—20th
century. 4. Germany—Social conditions—1918–1933.   I. Title.
II. Series.
DD256.5.F53   1995
943.085—dc20   94-23920

ISBN 0 7190 3502 3 *hardback*
        0 7190 3503 1 *paperback*

First published 1995

99 98 97 96 95   10 9 8 7 6 5 4 3 2 1

Photoset in Linotron Palatino
by Northern Phototypesetting Co. Ltd, Bolton

Printed in Great Britain
by Biddles Ltd, Guildford and King's Lynn

Contents

Introduction

In January 1919 German voters elected a National Assembly to draft a new constitution. In his opening address to the Assembly the Chancellor and future President of the Weimar Republic, Friedrich Ebert, alluded to the liberal values which had informed the revolutionaries of 1848 and declared that liberation from the constraints of the imperial era was imminent. However, as a defeated country the Germany of 1919 was not entirely master of its own fate, and whilst the US President, Woodrow Wilson, had anticipated a liberal, open international order in the post-war world, the eventual peace treaties were very different. The Weimar Republic became synonymous with national humiliation and confinement, and its liberal and democratic socialist aspirations were ultimately overwhelmed by a domestic opposition which took the 'shame' of the Versailles Treaty as its basic reference point. The National Socialists were the ultimate beneficiaries of Weimar's recurrent crises, but Hitler's rise to power was neither straightforward nor inevitable. There is a need to examine the key variables which led to his appointment as Chancellor on 30 January 1933.

As an opposition movement National Socialism displayed an alarming predisposition to violence and intolerance and purveyed a political message laced with anti-Semitic racialism. The worst fears of the opponents of the NSDAP (National Socialist German Workers' Party) were exceeded as Hitler's takeover unleashed a train of appalling events which have no equal in modern European history. This book, however, is not a history of the Third Reich and refrains from detailed comment on events postdating 30 January 1933. Nor is it a history of the Weimar Republic, for while National Socialism grew out of the republican, and earlier, periods of German history, it was synonymous with neither. The republican era displayed a range of noteworthy achievements which have contributed positively to the substance and ethos of contemporary Germany.

There is a massive and valuable literature on Nazism to which it is not possible to do justice in a brief introduction; a selection of key works and authors will be identified and discussed at appropriate points in the main text. Needless to say, the traumas of the Nazi era have triggered major debates over the origins and rise of National Socialism which, if acrimonious on occasion, have ultimately led to an accumulation of knowledge and a deepening of our understanding of the subject. Amid this, one thing has remained a constant: Nazism has found no advocate or defender among established academics or within the intellectual mainstream. Attempts to understand are one thing; to excuse or forgive would be quite another. Beyond this bedrock of common ground and understanding, areas of debate and controversy continue to develop, and in particular the common claim that National Socialism constituted in essence a middle-class *rassemblement* will be subjected here to close scrutiny.

The rise of the Nazis aims to be as accessible as possible to the new or general-interest reader and through its referencing of selected authors offers an entry to the wider literature. With this in mind the references are whenever possible to works written in or translated into English. The more specialised reader will find some of the subject matter familiar, but the underlying line of argument which is founded on recent and current research seeks to provide fresh insights into the rise of Nazism.

After setting the theme in a wider context and surveying the relationship between National Socialism and the established parties and institutions of Weimar, discussion focuses on the Nazis themselves. The ideological origins of Nazism, its programme and use of propaganda to project its message are examined, after which the creation of the Nazis' formidable, if brittle, organisational basis is considered. Following a discussion of what the Nazis were selling and how they tried to market their wares, attention turns to the potential customers, middle- and working-class, who supported the Nazis in varying measure and for reasons which were in part similar, in part very different. Hitler's contribution to the rise of National Socialism is accorded detailed attention within this framework.

Conclusions must follow from a consideration of the evidence and to betray them at the outset would be premature. However, in general terms it is hoped here to reconcile some of the more traditional explanations for the rise of Nazism with the most recent, not least through a reappraisal of the role and function of the concept of national solidarity within National Socialist ideology.

The grim consequences of this particular evocation of national solidarity make any study of Nazism a profoundly discomforting task. I am therefore very grateful to Jane Thorniley-Walker and Michelle O'Connell of Manchester University Press for their encouragement and advice during the drafting and production of this book and also to John Stevenson of Worcester College, Oxford, whose comments were much appreciated. Several colleagues in the Department of History at the University of Strathclyde also gave me more than my fair share of their time. Margaret Hastie provided an indispensable reconciliation service between myself and my word processor. Richard Finlay offered valuable suggestions in particular on the issue of nationalism, while James McMillan very generously read through and commented on the final text. Finally, I am grateful to Mary, Kate and Jane for their patience and understanding during the drafting of this book, for families suffer all the disadvantages and enjoy few of the benefits of this particular line of work.

1

The fall of Weimar

I

During the autumn of 1918 Germany's imperial order disintegrated. On 9 November the Emperor Wilhelm II abdicated
without nominating a successor. Military defeat had triggered
the final collapse of the monarchy, but a growing clamour for
constitutional reform and then the privations of war itself had
already eaten away at its inner substance. The imperial
authorities had not had a good war. The economy was mis-
handled and domestic policy generally was characterised by a
heavy-handedness which became increasingly malign and pronounced as the war progressed and the situation deteriorated.
The government pursued an all-or-nothing strategy in its foreign
policy, hoping in vain for a glorious victory which would justify
the slaughter and suffering, thereby restoring its credit and
silencing the reformists in Parliament and elsewhere. Military
successes did sustain the Empire well into 1918, but once the
military tide finally turned in July, failure quickly demanded its
price of the Emperor and the Army High Command.

The Social Democrats, who were trenchant advocates of political and social reform and had become increasingly critical of the
government's wartime policies, were the natural successors to
the imperial order. They were brought into government in
October 1918 to facilitate armistice negotiations with the United
States, and upon the abdication of the Emperor they took over the
administration. By this time Germany was in the grip of a popular
uprising, fuelled by outrage against the old order, which saw a
majority demanding a parliamentary republic and a minority an

ill-defined but more direct form of popular proletarian demo-cracy. There were widespread demands that the Empire's civil and military authorities be stripped of their powers and that heavy industry be nationalised. With regard to the constitution the pro-parliamentary majority was to prevail, and a reckoning was awaited with the old order which had unleashed the war, conducted it and lost it.

Elections to the constituent, National Assembly which were held on 19 January 1919 seemed to confirm the triumph of the revolution; parties dedicated to a pluralistic republican order polled over four fifths of the vote. Just eighteen months later, however, the first Reichstag elections of the Weimar era saw the pro-Weimar Social Democratic Party of Germany (SPD), Catholic Centre Party and German Democratic Party (DDP) poll just 43.6 per cent, although the Independent SPD won a further 20 per cent. Overall a shift to the right had begun which was to prevent the republican parties ever having a working majority in the Parliament they had created. In 1925 things reached the point where Field Marshal Paul von Hindenburg, one of the key figures in later wartime Germany and thus an architect of catastrophic defeat, was elected President of the Republic.

The course of the revolution itself is held to have prejudiced the Republic's prospects. The priorities of the majority Social Demo-crat, Friedrich Ebert, on accepting the office of Chancellor (Prime Minister) on 9 November 1918 were to restore a legal basis for government by arranging for the election of a constituent assembly, to address the disastrous economic situation, and to deal with the victorious Allies on the best terms available. He and his colleagues regarded the popular uprisings and demands for a role in government from the local councils of soldiers, sailors and workers as unwelcome and even threatening distractions. Ebert was particularly worried that the small, radical Spartakus League (which broke away from the Independent SPD and then joined with anarcho-syndicalists to form the Communist Party on 1 January 1919) might exploit the unrest and unleash civil war. To achieve his priorities and counter these threats he retained the imperial civil service, postponed any attempts to nationalise heavy industry and, most critically, agreed with army Quar-termaster General Groener to maintain the imperial army's officer corps in return for their assistance in crushing his enemies on the left. At the same time the trade unions, led by Carl Legien, reached a settlement of differences with the owners of heavy industry. The industrialists recognised the unions' sole right to bargain collectively industry by industry and to limited consultation within the workplace, and agreed to the eight-hour day; implicitly at least the unions had recognised the property rights of the industrialists by dealing with them in this way.

The radical left was dismayed by these compromises and some of their number staged an insurrection, dubbed the Spartakus Rising, in Berlin on 5 January. Despite its promises to Ebert, the army proved unreliable as a domestic gendarme and the Defence Minister Gustav Noske ordered volunteer units (*Freikorps*) of demobilised soldiers and some young civilians to restore order. They did so with great brutality, killing the Communist leaders Rosa Luxemburg and Karl Liebknecht among others, and thereby alienated the radical left from the Social Democrats for the duration of the Republic. During the 1950s, at the height of the Cold War, West German historians tended to condemn the radical left for forcing Ebert into co-operation with the imperial establishment, but more recently most have argued that his government over-reacted to a faction which represented little more than a nuisance. Whatever the case, decisions taken by Ebert's provisional government preserved intact key elements of the imperial establishment, allowing them to organise against the parliamentary republican order and in particular against Social Democratic participation in government.

The character of the peace settlement has also been regarded as prejudicial to the Republic's prospects. It was widely believed in Germany that the new, republican government would be treated leniently, according to the Fourteen Points formulated by US President Wilson in January 1918. The German government was prepared to make minor territorial concessions and to pay compensation for war damage to civilian property, but things turned out differently. The Allies, who had trouble enough agreeing among themselves on peace terms, did not negotiate openly with Germany, instead merely allowing limited written comment on a draft version of the treaty. The peace terms were liberal compared with Germany's own war aims, but territorial losses were substantial and reparations demands were open-ended. Furthermore, German public opinion felt that Article 231 of the treaty, which held their country responsible for war damage so as to provide a legal basis for reparations, was effectively moral condemnation of Germany as the party guilty for the war. From the 1960s onwards, research into the origins and conduct of the war has indicated that the imperial government should at least bear a large share of the responsibility for both, but the feeling was widespread in Weimar that the republicans, by signing the Treaty of Versailles in June 1919, had caved in cravenly to false accusations and demands. Many subsequently held the Social Democrats in particular responsible for the Republic's many problems which were believed to stem from the peace settlement.

The economy was a case in point. It had been left in a fragile state by the mobilisation of all available resources for the war effort. Millions of soldiers and war industry employees had to be re-directed into a peacetime economy (although many women were simply sacked as the men returned), a trade deficit grew as imports rose yet former export markets remained closed to German goods, and massive wartime borrowing left the new government saddled with a huge domestic debt. This debt unleashed inflation, but its effects were initially beneficial on balance. The war debt was rapidly eroded, and new borrowing to fund domestic expenditure and finance the trade deficit was made relatively painless. Private sector debts were also reduced and employers were able to agree high wage settlements with the powerful trade unions before passing on their additional costs in higher prices. The economy recovered rapidly, given the ready availability of credit, and by 1921 unemployment had virtually been eliminated. The rate of inflation increased further, but since the external value of the Reichmark fell more quickly than did its domestic value, German exporters became increasingly competitive and began to recapture lost markets.

Quite where this inflation-fuelled recovery would have led (and there were losers in the form of holders of liquid assets) is irrelevant because of the negative impact of the reparations problem. In April 1921 the Allies agreed on a bill of 132 billion gold marks, to be paid off at 2 billion gold marks annually, in addition to which 26 per cent of the value of annual German exports (a sum of 500 million gold marks) would be paid over each year. With a yearly trade deficit of around 1 billion gold marks, the German economy was faced with a total annual net loss of 3.5 billion marks at pre-war parity values. Since taxation did not even cover domestic expenditure, the government was forced to borrow from the Reichsbank and then buy hard foreign currency with these rapidly devaluing marks to meet reparations demands. The actual payment of reparations occurred in the form of German goods (bought with the borrowed money) or hard currency.

As the main western victim of German aggression and the chief recipient of reparations, the French became increasingly uneasy. Deliveries of German goods were a mixed blessing, for they often displaced the markets of French industry. The cash payments were more welcome, but since Germany raised the sums by dumping its own depreciating currency, the process devalued the mark further and made German exports even more competitive. Growing French exasperation was compounded by the effects of US foreign policy. In March 1920 the Senate had washed its hands of the Versailles Treaty and in August 1921 the USA signed a separate peace with Germany. It also stayed out-with the League of Nations which France perceived as a guarantor of the post-war settlement. Fearful of German economic recovery and its own increasing military and diplo-matic isolation, France invaded the Ruhr District on 11 January 1923 – ostensibly to extract reparations by force, but in the hope eventually of detaching the Rhine territories from Germany.

At once the issue of Germany's domestic fortunes merged with the reparations question and thus with the terms of the Versailles Treaty. The loss of the Ruhr's economy and the financial costs of underwriting a campaign of passive resistance in the occupied area triggered Germany's infamous hyperinflation which saw private savings utterly destroyed. The human costs of the passive resistance were borne by the working classes and junior civil servants of the Ruhr (the bourgeois parties refused to sanction additional taxes on their constituents to fund the campaign), but general anger mounted against the Weimar Republic for its agreement to sign the peace terms which had led first to the reparations demands of 1921 and now apparently to the disaster of 1923. Social tensions also grew during the summer, bringing down the pro-business minority government of Wilhelm Cuno, but a broad coalition of the SPD, Centre, DDP and DVP (German People's Party) led by Gustav Stresemann defused labour unrest, moved to settle with France and to stabilise the currency. As the objective situation took a turn for the better the radical anti-republican forces finally moved to exploit the legacy of the crisis in order to topple Weimar. On 12 and 13 October Communist leaders gained ministerial posts within the left-wing SPD administrations of Saxony and Thuringia, hoping to obtain police weapons for a rising. The army intervened on 21 October and deposed the governments, thereby precipitating the resignation of Social Democratic ministers from the national government. Although the SPD did not sanction the plans of the German Communist Party (KPD) for a rising, they had sought co-operation with the Communists and noted that while the army had acted decisively against the left, it held back from intervening in Bavaria where more or less open treason was brewing. The Social Democrats were not to re-enter government until June 1928 and were therefore out of office during the relatively stable middle years of the Republic when constructive reform was a possibility and the task of governance was altogether less punishing than before or afterwards.

The Bavarian crisis marked the last attempt at open insurrection by right-wing paramilitary forces, but their list of earlier outrages was long. The engagement of *Freikorps* units on Germany's eastern frontier had not been particularly controversial and the Upper Silesian campaign of mid-1921 had even won plaudits from elements of the Communist Party. The *Freikorps'* role in domestic politics, however, was an entirely different matter. During the early days of the Republic, it must be said, their existence was considered indispensable by both the army chiefs and the government. Although General Groener had promised to uphold domestic order, his commanders found that regular troops were unwilling to re-enact the slaughter of the western front in the towns and cities of Germany. Only the *Freikorps* enabled the army chiefs to honour their promise to the government, albeit by proxy, and thereby secure for the High Command a longer-term role within the Republic. And it was only because of the *Freikorps* (or so it seemed to Defence Minister Noske and his government colleagues) that Germany had not disintegrated in chaos during 1919.

The *Freikorps* put down left-wing disorder with considerable harshness. Following the failure of the Spartakus Rising in January 1919, sporadic popular unrest and *Freikorps* brutality fed upon one another for several months. The paramilitary units seized every opportunity to strike down insurgents or strikers whom they regarded as treacherous class warriors inspired (or so they believed) as often as not by Jewish agitators of indeterminate nationality. Linkages with the vocabulary and ideology of Nazism are very much apparent.

The *Freikorps'* most critical campaign was launched in March 1920, but this time the government was their target. In compliance with the peace terms the authorities had begun to disband military units, including elements of the *Freikorps*. Fearing for their future, paramilitary forces stationed outside Berlin needed little prompting from conservative conspirators to march on the capital and displace the government. A rebel administration led by a civil servant, Wolfgang Kapp, only lasted a few days before being toppled by a general strike and the best prospects during the Weimar era for a decisive reckoning with the old order had presented themselves. Not only had the *Freikorps* openly demonstrated their contempt for the republican order, but senior army commanders had disloyally refused to support their commander, General Reinhardt, and crush the coup. Furthermore the wartime Chief of Staff, General Ludendorff, had been involved in the *Putsch*, thereby placing the bona fides of the military caste even further in doubt.

The striking workers expected the government to seize the initiative and purge the army officer corps, replace outspoken monarchists within the higher echelons of the civil service, and look again at prospects for nationalising heavy industry. Instead the Socialist-Catholic coalition promoted General von Seeckt (who had not opposed the *Putsch*) to army commander and was consequently faced with open insurgency in parts of the Ruhr District and central Germany. In an act of unintended irony the government unleashed the *Freikorps* on the insurgents and deepened still further the bitter mistrust between radical left-wingers and mainstream Social Democracy. Furthermore the Kapp *Putsch* and its bloody aftermath left General von Seeckt free to proclaim the army's independence from politics. By this was meant detachment from and indifference towards the republican constitutional order. The army considered itself loyal to the German State, but not specifically to the Republic, and during the early 1930s this loyalty to 'Germany' was to trigger active conspiracy against Weimar.

While *Freikorps* units wrought havoc on a mass scale, secret societies and prominent members of the old establishment also inflicted great damage on the Republic. Leading politicians, including the Bavarian Minister President Kurt Eisner, the retired national Finance Minister Matthias Erzberger and Foreign Minister Walther Rathenau, were assassinated by right-wing terror groups. Of individuals, Field Marshal von Hindenburg did particular damage when, in November 1919, he declared to a government commission that elements within Germany had engineered the country's defeat. This 'stab-in-the-back' legend fed on widespread public resentment over defeat and, still more, the Allies' subsequent treatment of Germany. It was a relatively short step from the general accusation that Germany had been stabbed in the back to the more specific contention that the republicans had brought defeat on the country and that, had the imperial army been allowed to prosecute the war unopposed, then Germany would have won. The assertion that Germany divided (allegedly by Jews) had lost, but that Germany united was invincible was to inform and make credible the National Socialists' rhetoric in the realm of foreign policy.

Although the national government was restored to power in Berlin after the Kapp *Putsch*, the Social Democratic administration in Bavaria was not so lucky. A reactionary, particularist and clericist government took office and provided sanctuary for right-wing extremists of every sort as the military and civil authorities elsewhere in Germany finally moved to marginalise them. The ensuing alliance between the radical right and the Bavarian authorities was one of convenience. In pursuit of their particularist goals Bavaria and its armed forces displayed increasing insubordination to Berlin and sought to mobilise right-wing paramilitaries in support of their objectives. An army captain, Ernst Röhm, played a vital intermediary role between the authorities and the radical right, especially the NSDAP of which he was a member, but the Nazi leader Adolf Hitler aspired to exploit the Bavarian situation as a springboard for a national revolution.

Matters came to a head in November 1923. Relations between Munich and Berlin had reached a very low ebb and on 9 November Hitler tried to seize control of all the dissident groupings in Munich as a prelude to a 'march on Berlin'. The

Bavarian authorities were not Nazis, nor did they wish to seize Berlin. The police fired on Hitler's demonstration just north of Munich's city centre and his attempt to emulate Mussolini ended in farce. The ensuing trial was a farce of a very different sort. Hitler was duly charged with high treason and appeared in court in February 1924 along with co-conspirators who included Röhm and Ludendorff, the latter having escaped unscathed from his earlier involvement in the Kapp *Putsch*. Hitler's fellow defendants were acquitted, but he was found guilty and sentenced to five years (relatively commodious) imprisonment in the fortress of Landsberg. During the trial Hitler made plain the Bavarian authorities' complicity in the events leading to 9 November and was allowed free rein to unleash a withering attack on the Republic and its foreign policy. Far from appearing a dilettante blunderer Hitler went to prison a martyr and authoritative spokesman for Germany's radical right. As for the Bavarian government, Hitler's *Putsch* had short-circuited its own preparations openly to confront the Republic and it subsided into embarrassed silence, unpunished by Berlin.

The apparent pusillanimity of the republican authorities resulted in part from their vulnerability to hostile institutional forces and partly from growing popular enmity. Although General von Seeckt had been swift to move against left-wing Saxony and Thuringia in October 1923, he was unsure how to handle the Bavarian crisis and his Bavarian counterpart General von Lossow. The Bavarian courts were not unique in displaying leniency towards right-wing rebels and terrorists; it was the same elsewhere and left-wingers, by contrast, were sometimes as likely to be shot out-of-hand as to come to court at all. The Republic was also absorbed with the substantial problems of currency stabilisation, reparations and re-establishing tolerable relations with France in particular. And public opinion was turning decisively against the Republic at the polls. In May 1924 the republican SPD, DDP and Centre between them won just 39.6 per cent of the vote in Reichstag elections as the anti-republican left and right were greatly strengthened, with the radical *völkisch* coalition (which included elements of the NSDAP) taking 6.5 per cent. Matters improved slightly for the republican parties in further elections in December 1924, but following the death of President Ebert in 1925 Field Marshal von Hindenburg won the ensuing elections as the anti-republican candidate.

It is not surprising that many Germans had turned on the republican parties, given the traumatic upheavals of Weimar's early years, but it might appear perverse at best that they turned in large numbers to right-wing parties which were associated to a greater or lesser degree with the failed imperial order. Here the ambivalent impact of the war played an important role. The killing and slaughter were not remembered with any fondness and it is significant that both Ernst Röhm when Chief of Staff of the *Sturmabteilung* (SA) and, initially, Hitler when Chancellor were careful to denounce in public any thought of another shooting war. Against that the virtues of national solidarity in wartime and in particular of male solidarity in the trenches were contrasted with the fractiousness of civil politics. The most obvious fragmentation existed within the conservative and liberal camps, but the republicans and in particular the Social Democrats were accused of doubtful loyalty to the nation and of pursuing sectional objectives. The right in general succeeded in assuming the mantle of the guardian of collective national interests, while the National Socialists were to add to this demands for societal reform so as to strengthen national cohesion.

II

The attitude one adopts towards the middle, 'golden', years of the Weimar Republic is a matter of perspective. Intellectual and cultural achievements in the arts and sciences made a decisive and (thanks to the defeat of Nazism) enduring contribution to the character of contemporary Germany and, indeed, the world. Social legislation and reform gave Weimar the appearance of an advanced and progressive society and again provided models for post-Second World War society. The economy fared better and the reparations issue was defused to a degree by the Dawes Plan (1924) and Young Plan (1929). In its wider foreign policy the Republic found a skilled advocate in Gustav Stresemann who blended reconciliation with the West with a subtle brand of *Realpolitik* which has led historians to probe his ultimate motives ever since. The Locarno Settlement of 1925 and Germany's subsequent admission to the League of Nations in 1926, coupled with the gradual evacuation of occupied territory by the Allies, were a world apart from the atmosphere that had prevailed in 1919.

Unfortunately, however, it is not possible to dwell on achievements that provided the Republic with breathing space when setting the scene for the rise of the Nazis. Even during the 'golden' years there were many indications of trouble to come.

In the socio-economic field Germany's heavy industrial magnates were prominent among the opponents of Weimar. They had been glad of trade union co-operation during the revolutionary crisis, but even by the early 1920s moves were afoot to (re-)kindle a corporate spirit within individual factories which opposed full-square Weimar's class-based labour relations and social policy. There were disagreements between the heavy industrialists and their colleagues in manufacturing and light industry over whether to allow the trade unions a role in the economy at all, but even the moderates foresaw a corporatist role for the unions bereft of any class-political objectives. The unemployment insurance scheme of 1927 was regarded as an unacceptable addition to unit labour costs (although gains in productivity had outstripped wage rises during Weimar). Proposals by the SPD and trade unions in 1928 that worker participation in the management of companies should serve as the prelude to some form of social ownership (the Naphtali Programme) were seen as the last straw.

The Social Democrats themselves have attracted criticism for their stand-offish attitude to participation in national government during the 'golden' years. Prussia remained a Social Democratic bastion, but central government coalitions saw the republican interest represented basically by the Centre Party. A variety of factors conditioned the SPD's stance, some ideological, others strategic. In 1921 at Görlitz the Social Democrats had subscribed to a programme which promoted parliamentary republican values, saw the SPD participating in a pluralistic political order and advocated social solidarity in the national context rather than class solidarity. At Heidelberg in 1925 the party changed its official line. By then a large part of the Independent SPD had rejoined the majority party, bringing with it older notions of class struggle and the ultimate victory of socialism which looked back to the nineteenth-century Erfurt Programme. Leading intellectuals in the party, including the former Independent Rudolf Hilferding, continued to argue that a democratic political order possessed virtues in its own right, but this could not suppress the ambivalence created at Heidelberg, which was reinforced by a reluctance among the SPD's trade union colleagues to see it in coalition. The Social Democrats also had strategic reasons for adopting a more forthrightly socialist stance. Part of the Independent SPD had joined the KPD at the end of 1920 and the greatly strengthened Communists had polled 12.6 per cent in the May 1924 Reichstag election to the SPD's 20.5 per cent. Despite a recovery in the SPD's fortunes in December, and a decline in the KPD's vote, there remained a nagging fear in Social Democratic circles that too great a readiness to compromise with the 'bourgeois' parties would cost it votes and members. It was almost impossible thereafter for the SPD to square the circle between maintaining ideological purity and functioning as a party of government in a beleaguered system which it had done most to create.

Politicians on the left of the Centre Party, such as Josef Wirth, became increasingly concerned by the SPD's isolationism. It undermined efforts to maintain a strong republican presence in coalition governments and also removed any brake on a rightward drift within the Centre Party itself. The Centre was continually in government, but with the small left-liberal DDP and Stresemann's larger right-liberal DVP. The conservative DNVP (German National People's Party) also participated in some coalitions, all of which lent greater authority to figures in the Centre Party who subscribed to more traditional and con-servative Catholic values. In 1925 Wirth proposed that a Republican Union be created, to include the SPD, Centre, DDP and the republican paramilitary league, the Reichsbanner Schwarz Rot Gold. At this stage there was still active support for such a notion in the Centre Party, but the DDP and, more crucially, the SPD showed sufficient reserve to kill the plan.

In spite of itself the SPD could scarcely avoid office after the elections of May 1928. Having polled almost 30 per cent, it formed the heart of a coalition with a working majority and led by the Social Democrat Hermann Müller, but the apparent calm of the mid-1920s quickly disintegrated. During 1928 labour relations in the Ruhr District collapsed and the resulting strikes and lockouts further convinced the industrialists, if they needed more prompt-ing, that the constitutional order was suspect. The State's role in labour relations exacerbated this situation. Legislation had provided for State arbitration where differences between employers and trade unions proved unbridgeable, and an increasing recourse to this arbitration accompanied by growing unhappiness at the compromises imposed made the connection between industrial relations and the constitution explicit.

Far greater problems emerged in the areas of foreign policy and finance. As mentioned, the Foreign Minister Gustav Stresemann had done much to rehabilitate Germany from 1924 onward and in 1929 proposals further to relax reparations conditions, the Young Plan, were accepted by German negotiators. Stresemann's overall strategy had revealed considerable subtlety and skill. Never exceeding the bounds of the possible, he had exploited Germany's inherent economic strength. He had also exploited differences between the Allied powers while meeting their aspirations where no great sacrifice was demanded on his own part. Through his connections with the business world Stresemann understood that Franco-German economic cooperation offered many more advantages than sterile confrontation and he cultivated links with French business and politicians to this end. However, he had always maintained cordial relations with Moscow as a counterweight to his western strategy and tolerated his army's secret rearmament programme in the Soviet Union. At the end of the day the victor powers received binding guarantees of German good behaviour in the West, but were forced to acknowledge the prospect of an eventual territorial revision in the East as well as growing German economic influence in Eastern and South-eastern Europe.

The right found the western dimension of his foreign policy unforgivable. Just as the Weimar constitution had reined in their domestic powers, so Stresemann's foreign policy accepted limitations to German power in Europe. If the worst consequences of defeat had been removed, the Foreign Minister seemed equally to have renounced any prospect of Germany dominating the entire continent. In early 1929 the monarchist paramilitary league, the Stahlhelm, suggested a referendum on the constitution which proposed that the President nominate his own cabinet free from parliamentary control. Even the DNVP was not keen, despite certain similarities between these proposals and the former imperial constitution, but when the Stahlhelm's leader, Theodor

Duesterberg, switched his attack to foreign policy he quickly found allies among the parties. The DNVP had come under the control of an industrialist and press magnate, Alfred Hugenberg, who offended some of the party's old guard, but succeeded in steering it onto a more radical and aggressive anti-republican course. He perceived Duesterberg's scheme, to demand a referendum on the Young Plan, as a means of attacking the Weimar constitution as a whole. The other party political ally, the NSDAP, appeared a less important catch, but Hitler's acknowledged abilities as a public speaker and his party's populist character were useful additions to the campaign. It quickly became apparent that Hugenberg and Hitler had very different objectives. The former sought through the campaign to create a National Solidarity Movement which would outlast the referendum and become an organisational focus for the 'national' forces in German politics; the latter simply wished to exploit the widespread publicity afforded to the NSDAP through Hugenberg's newspapers and as far as possible present his party as the key participant in the referendum struggle.

Hitler's strategy was more successful. The NSDAP did indeed gain valuable publicity and acquired a fair measure of respectability, while the modest 5.8 million votes cast for the Solidarity Movement's referendum proposals represented a humiliation for Hugenberg. The problem had focused on his inability to mobilise the entire right, for in branding Weimar's foreign policy as treason he implicitly attacked President von Hindenburg as well as the DVP; even the old guard within the DNVP itself distanced itself from his stridency. However, the right in general felt the time was ripe to address the constitutional question and the earlier election of von Hindenburg as President was soon to be crucial.

III

The worsening economic situation triggered the slide towards some form or another of authoritarian government. Germany's economic recovery had been hesitant and patchy during the mid-1920s and a good deal of public spending, the funding of the trade deficit and reparations, and even the servicing of an accumulating debt itself were covered by borrowing, particularly from the US private sector. The continuance of these loans depended on Germany remaining a good risk and above that a tempting haven for foreign investment by virtue of especially generous interest rates. Changes in US monetary policy in 1928 and then the crash of 1929 ended all that. The German economy went into a precipitate decline which soon burdened the social security budget very heavily indeed. The SPD was as staunch an advocate of economic orthodoxy as any other party and agreed that social security spending had to be balanced against revenue, but it disagreed with its coalition partners over how to achieve this. The Social Democrats and trade unions favoured an additional levy on employers, but their coalition partners, including the DVP which had close links with industry, proposed benefit cuts or an additional contribution from employees. The Centre Party politician, Heinrich Brüning, tried to override sectional interests by suggesting a compromise between cuts and higher revenue, which was accepted by non-socialist members of the coalition, but rejected by the SPD after some deliberation. In March Müller resigned as Chancellor, the Social Democrats left government for the last time, and although they could not possibly have foreseen the scale of the forthcoming disaster, events which led ultimately to Hitler's appointment as Chancellor had been set in train.

As Brüning replaced Müller the Nazis were far from his mind. He wished to end reparations payments once and for all and partly as a means to this end pursued orthodox, deflationary economic policies. This strategy intensified material hardship in a country already deep in recession, and a reliable parliamentary majority became indispensable if Brüning's tough line was to succeed. However, hopes that the non-Marxist majority in the Reichstag would support the government turned out to be false; Hugenberg maintained a firm grip on the DNVP and distanced himself from the Chancellor, necessitating early elections in September 1930. Brüning hoped for a decisive switch in public mood towards the concept of a 'national' government, standing increasingly above parties and relying ultimately on the President rather than Parliament for its authority. In the event there was a bigger shift in popular sentiment than he had bargained for. The Catholic parties (Centre and Bavarian People's Party, or BVP) more or less held their ground, but the other conventional parties of the centre and right, as well as the SPD, took a battering. The Communist Party profited to a degree, but the National Socialists were the main beneficiaries. The surge in their share of the vote from 2.6 per cent (1928) to 18.3 per cent owed much to desertions from Brüning's putative centre-right bloc.

Many establishment figures hoped that the new-found popular strength of the radical NSDAP might eventually be harnessed for more conservative nationalist goals, but others, including von Hindenburg and Defence Minister Groener, were deeply suspicious of Hitler's movement in general and the paramilitary SA in particular. Furthermore Hitler showed no inclination to serve in a coalition, and his 107 Reichstag deputies, far from facilitating the formation of a non-Marxist bloc actually hindered this. The consequences were deeply ironic in a number of ways. Having welcomed the SPD's departure from government in March, Brüning now relied on its goodwill to conduct parliamentary business. The Social Democrats themselves, having ducked the responsibility for painful compromise in early 1930, now tolerated a deflationary economic strategy which included severe cuts in welfare benefits. They also accepted a growing propensity for rule by emergency presidential decree under Article 48 of the constitution. This article, originally designed to furnish a republican President with additional powers in an emergency, was now being used by a monarchist President and his entourage to conduct day-to-day business and thereby move Germany away from a republican parliamentary system of government towards an as yet undefined system of authoritarian rule.

The SPD justified its stance as toleration of the 'lesser evil', Hitler being the greater, but experience of Brüning's 'lesser evil' brought increasing numbers of Germans to the end of their tether. Registered unemployment eventually exceeded 30 per cent and it has been estimated that half the economically active population was effectively without work during the winters of 1931–32 and 1932–33. Many thousands of small family firms went to the wall; smaller farms went bankrupt as what help the authorities could provide for agriculture benefited the politically influential, larger landowners in the main. Diseases associated with the worst periods of wartime famine reappeared; tuberculosis and pneumonia, infant mortality and death in childbirth ravaged a weakened, malnourished population. As parents lost their jobs or faced bankruptcy and ruin, their older children found life at home economically impossible or emotionally unbearable and left – to wander the streets or the countryside in search of any plausible escape from their desperation (see Document 33). Of those fortunate enough to retain a living, many saw incomes cut and the fear hung over them and over the remaining pockets of reasonable prosperity that the tide of misery and want would ultimately overwhelm them. By July 1932 in Reichstag elections 37.4 per cent of voters were prepared to support the Nazis and a further 14.5 per cent the Communists, giving the radical anti-republican parties a blocking majority in Parliament.

In late 1930, however, neither von Hindenburg nor Brüning desired to remain reliant on Social Democratic goodwill. One possible longer-term solution was to 'tame' the NSDAP in accordance with the national goals of the right, but the immediate strategy led to a decline in the influence of Parliament. Brüning's administration lent greater powers to senior civil servants and used Article 48 with growing impunity and increasingly independently of the Reichstag. If legislation was still presented to Parliament it came in opaque, legalistic form. By 1932 Parliament came to meet on just thirteen days, to pass five laws, although it retained the important negative capacity to pass a vote of no confidence in the government of the day. In the same year sixty-nine emergency decrees were proclaimed. In October 1931, on von Hindenburg's insistence, Brüning carried out a cabinet reshuffle which took its composition significantly further to the right. Not only did the new cabinet include people who were actively hostile to the constitution, but, as Hans Mommsen observes, von Hindenburg had influenced the political composition of the cabinet without reference to the balance of forces in Parliament; a *de facto* shift in the constitutional balance of power towards the President was unmistakable.[1]

The point had probably been passed at which the Republic could be saved, although the Social Democrats and trade unions still hoped that an improvement in the economic climate would restore their political fortunes and hence the health of Weimar itself. Others were already scrapping for their share in the inheritance. On 11 October 1931 those right-wing parties outwith the government (notably the DNVP and NSDAP) and also extra-parliamentary leagues such as the Stahlhelm and the Pan-

Germans held a convention at the spa town of Bad Harzburg at which they announced the formation of the Harzburg Front. The constellation of forces assembled there resembled those which placed Hitler in the Chancellor's office in January 1933, but at Bad Harzburg these participants were united around their opposition to the Brüning cabinet and the Republic rather than around any common programme or positive strategy. Hitler participated grudgingly and absented himself from significant parts of the proceedings, indicating that while Hugenberg and company might need him, he did not necessarily need them (see Document 3). An SA rally held just days later in Brunswick, involving around 70,000 storm-troopers from all over Germany, was a clear demonstration of the National Socialists' own strength if any such were still needed. Furthermore, key elements of the anti-republican camp had been missing at Bad Harzburg; industry had little time for Hugenberg and remained wary of Hitler while Defence Minister Groener appeared to retain the full loyalty of senior army commanders.

Behind the scenes, however, both leading industrialists and army chiefs were prepared to listen to what Hitler had to say; and although these meetings, such as Hitler's address to the Düsseldorf Industry Club in January 1932, did little to eliminate their equivocal attitudes towards Nazism, they remained confronted by its growing popularity and strength. Groener's protegé, General von Schleicher, who had the ear of von Hindenburg, contemplated harnessing the NSDAP's strength in order to eliminate the SPD as a political force before turning on the Nazis themselves. His order of priorities was more or less representative of the right's attitude at this stage and spoke volumes. Hitler was under no illusions regarding the right's ultimate goodwill and was determined to use the approaching state elections of 1932 and, if possible, presidential and national elections further to cash in on his movement's popularity and thereby strengthen his hand. The rules of the game were at once complex and very simple. The anti-republican right sought Hitler's backing to destroy the Republic on their terms, while the Nazi leader sought their backing to do the same on his. For the moment, however, von Hindenburg and Brüning were caught in the unpalatable situation of relying on Social Democratic goodwill to continue the business of government in the face of Nazi and DNVP opposition.

These bizarre battle lines became more clearly drawn in early 1932 when Hitler and Hugenberg individually refused to allow an extension of von Hindenburg's term as President. Presidential elections were duly called and on the second ballot von Hindenburg secured his tenure with 53 per cent of the vote. However, he found his situation unenviable. On 22 February Hitler had announced his own candidature, spurring the DNVP and Stahlhelm to put up Duesterberg for the old right. The Communist Party offered its leader, Ernst Thälmann, to the electorate, leaving von Hindenburg supported by the SPD, the Catholic parties and various remnants of the political middle, forces for which he had no time and whom he wished removed from any positions of power. Hitler had polled a creditable 37 per cent after a vigorous campaign conducted by Joseph Goebbels which extolled his personal virtues as the putative saviour of Germany. Disappointment within the Nazi movement over his failure to win was suppressed by sweeping advances in subsequent state elections (the NSDAP eclipsed the SPD in Prussia) and the prospect of fresh national elections.

These were occasioned by the resignation of Brüning and the failure of his successor, Franz von Papen, to obtain the necessary vote of confidence in the Reichstag. In April the State governments, led by Prussia, finally forced the central government to act against the Nazi paramilitaries who were a menace to law and order (see Documents 1 and 29–31) and, it appeared, were formulating plans to seize power unlawfully if circumstances demanded or permitted. On 13 April the Defence and Interior Minister, Groener, announced a ban on the SA and SS (*Schutzstaffel*) with, he believed, the full backing of senior army chiefs. However, he must have been aware that some regional army commands had been providing units and individual members of the SA with training for over a year (see Document 2). Moreover, in a betrayal of personal trust and friendship, General von Schleicher argued that to ban just the Nazi leagues while tolerating the continued existence of the republican Reichsbanner was to display partisanship, and this view was shared by much of the right. The argument was a nonsense on several grounds. The obvious counterpoint to the SA was the Communist Red Front which had been banned (by the Social

Democrats) years earlier. Furthermore the Reichsbanner was dedicated to upholding, not undermining, the existing constitutional order and refrained by and large from aggressive violence.

Such arguments were of little interest to the conservative opposition, however, and von Hindenburg was quickly persuaded to dismiss Brüning on 30 May; the earlier resignation of Groener had not saved him. The departing Chancellor had some grounds for bitterness, for as Germany was racked by the progressive collapse of her financial system in mid-1931 the US government moved first to suspend reparations and then in December to note expert advice that further payments were pointless. The formal ending of reparations came in July 1932 at the Lausanne Conference, but Brüning had effectively achieved his prime aim and almost survived long enough in office to see the beginnings of economic recovery. On the other hand, he had been instrumental in ushering in a significant presidential role in government, which ultimately destroyed him, while downgrading the importance of the Reichstag where, with SPD toleration, he still had a majority.

Von Schleicher had played a major part in the destruction of Brüning's administration and now did much to fashion the political landscape in which his successor, Franz von Papen, would operate. He sought to consolidate a conservative, authoritarian regime as effectively as possible, to which end National Socialist support in Parliament appeared indispensable. Von Schleicher, who had entered von Papen's cabinet as Defence Minister, had for some time entertained the notion that by involving the Nazis in affairs of state they might, indeed, be tamed. Discussions with Hitler elicited a promise of support for von Papen, but on condition that the SA ban was lifted and fresh Reichstag elections held. Along the road to these elections von Papen suspended the minority Socialist government of Prussia and installed himself as State Commissioner with decree powers, thus removing the SPD's last significant foothold in the governance of Germany and setting a precedent for the Nazis' overthrow of state administrations in early 1933.

No doubt to his disappointment, but fully in accordance with electoral trends, the Reichstag elections of 31 July delivered derisory support to von Papen and made Hitler's toleration of his beleaguered minority government essential. Hitler himself had sought an outright mandate and although the 37.3 per cent polled by the NSDAP fell well short of that, it left him with a stranglehold on German political life. The Nazis won 230 of the 608 seats in Parliament and the remaining seats were held by hopelessly divided and estranged political blocs. Hitler therefore intimated that in these changed (but predictable) circumstances he should form an administration himself. Von Papen resisted this suggestion and at a meeting with von Hindenburg on 13 August the Nazi leader found the President emphatic that the former should remain as Chancellor. The best offer Hitler received was the post of Vice Chancellor, and his refusal of this brought about a period of political stalemate.

Feelers between the NSDAP and the Centre Party, which had moved to the right under the leadership of Ludwig Kaas, appeared to offer a parliamentary solution to the crisis, for the two parties between them had 305 of the 608 Reichstag seats. However, leaving aside Hitler's thoroughly negative view of parliamentarianism, von Hindenburg and von Papen were deter-mined to work towards a presidential solution to the crisis. Rebuffed by a massive vote of no confidence in the Reichstag on 12 September, von Papen toyed with the idea of dissolving Parlia-ment indefinitely, but eventually called fresh elections. Held on 6 November, these saw the NSDAP lose thirty-four seats, but with 196 in a parliament of 584 deputies its strength remained decisive and von Papen was no nearer to winning a vote of confidence.

He tried to persuade von Hindenburg to sanction an authoritarian *coup d'état*, but von Schleicher and the army com-mand argued against this on practical grounds. The Reichswehr, they claimed, would have been unable to deal with an ensuing civil war and with any attempt by the Polish army to exploit subsequent German weakness on the eastern frontier. Instead von Schleicher proposed that he would form a government with sufficient popular backing to survive a vote of confidence and was duly appointed Chancellor on 2 December. The messy events of the following two months revolved around three factions and their ambitions: von Schleicher who struggled vainly to gain majority support in the Reichstag, Hitler who refused to compromise on his demand for the Chancellorship despite the setback of 6 November, and the old right who became increas-ingly alarmed at von Schleicher's tactics.

The Chancellor understood that despite Hitler's intransigence, his Chief of National Organisation, Gregor Strasser, was more and more inclined to secure a role for the NSDAP within a modified Weimar system. Von Schleicher offered Strasser the role of Vice Chancellor in a coalition which also sought to harness Centre Party, trade union and Social Democratic support for policies which acknowledged business interests, but also proposed a job creation programme and deficit spending. For the plan to succeed it was essential that Strasser bring a significant number of Nazi deputies with him, but once Hitler had angrily denounced the deal Strasser backed down, resigned his party offices and left politics altogether. In mid-1934, during the purge of the SA's leadership, he was to be killed on Hitler's orders for what the latter regarded as an outright betrayal.

In the shorter term von Schleicher was left without support in the Reichstag and facing his former conservative colleagues and a President who viewed his overtures to the left with deep suspicion. He himself had convinced von Hindenburg that a state of emergency was not an option just weeks earlier, which made his own request for such a step futile. By now the old right had boxed itself in completely. The NSDAP and KPD continued to possess a negative blocking majority in the Reichstag which prevented the formation of any coalition which excluded both of them. The inclusion of the KPD in government was, of course, unthinkable, which left Hitler in a far stronger position than his party's declining electoral fortunes suggested. With attempts to conduct government through the executive in defiance of the Reichstag's wishes at a dead end, von Hindenburg was eventually persuaded in late January to meet Hitler's demands. He was appointed Chancellor on 30 January, albeit within a cabinet dominated by conservative ministers. These conservatives had repeatedly demonstrated the extent of their destructive ineptitude over the preceding years and they did not disappoint Hitler on this score in early 1933.

It swiftly became clear that Hitler was exploiting the conservatives and not they him, despite von Papen's pathetic boast to the contrary as he assumed the post of Vice Chancellor in Hitler's first cabinet. The army chiefs tolerated Hitler's appointment, the great landowners of eastern Germany and the industrialists of the west found the prospect of a National Socialist-led administration altogether less menacing than the prospect of a return of the SPD. If, in accordance with its democratic principles, the SPD had carried out its revolution hestitantly and even half-heartedly in 1918 and 1919, Hitler was not troubled by any such scruples in 1933. On 1 February the Reichstag was dissolved as a series of emergency decrees (which paid lip-service to conservative-nationalist values) began to destroy the checks and balances which the constitution and the civil code had placed in the way of dictatorship. On 5 March the NSDAP polled 44 per cent in the last elections of the Weimar era, its allies in the DNVP 8 per cent. Hitler, however, was not concerned with the conduct of affairs through a parliamentary majority. The State governments were eliminated during early March, and on 23 March Hitler obtained the necessary two-thirds majority in the Reichstag to pass the Enabling Act. The Centre Party, with 11.2 per cent of the vote, and the gaggle of smaller right-wing parties, with 8.4 per cent, had no wish to make things difficult for the new Chancellor and voted for the Act which abolished the Reichstag in its old form and concentrated power in the hands of the government. Only the SPD opposed the move, the Communists having already been excluded from a Parliament which they, too, had hoped to destroy. The subsequent liquidation of the trade unions, the purging of the civil service and the official pronouncement of the one-party State on 14 July 1933 completed the consolidation of the National Socialists in power. Weimar had indeed been destroyed, but on very different terms from those envisaged by von Hindenburg and Brüning in 1930, or even by von Papen in January 1933.

Note

1 Hans Mommsen, *Die verspielte Freiheit. Der Weg der Republik von Weimar in den Untergang 1918 bis 1933*, Frankfurt-am-Main, Berlin, 1990, pp. 404–6.

2

The ideological basis of Nazism

I

The ideological basis of National Socialism continues to attract
intense scrutiny from historians, political and social scientists.
Over the years it has sometimes been perceived as a major sub-set
of a broader ideology, whether fascist or totalitarian. The proposition that Nazism was a type of fascism continues to attract
support from a broad range of historians who are able to identify
characteristics which it and Italian fascism shared in common,
such as a dynamic radical nationalism, the strong leader, the
one-party State, an advocacy of masculinity and of communal as
against individualist values. They can also identify common
origins, such as mounting crisis within the capitalist industrial
order, great hostility to this order within residual, but powerful,
pre-industrial elements of society, the legacy of failure in the First
World War and the challenge posed to national solidarity by
class-based, Marxist revolutionary movements. The proposition
that Nazism shared essential common characteristics with other
totalitarian regimes, including the Marxist-Leninist order in the
Soviet Union, found its most capable and eloquent advocates
during the Cold War era. At other times historians have argued
that National Socialism was unique. The enormous impact of
Hitler on Nazi ideology, leading to its description as Hitlerism, or
alternatively the fundamental importance to it of biological
racialism (not echoed in Italian fascism) are regarded as the
decisive factors in this literature.

Few, if any, writers have been 'disinterested parties' but have
sought instead either to save something of German history and

society from the moral wreckage of Nazism, or to define and investigate the culpable parties. The most narrowly focused studies have depicted Nazism either as a product of Hitler's own ideas and objectives or as the consequence of aberrant, relatively untypical currents in German history, thereby largely exonerating the country's institutions and elites. At the other extreme some non-German writers who were active during and just after the war perceived National Socialist ideology and foreign policy as a logical consequence of Germany's past and regarded 'Germany' and not 'Hitler' as the fundamental problem. A. J. P. Taylor's famous polemical work, *The Course of German History*, in which he remarked that 'the Germans sought freedom in the conquest of others',[1] was a notable example of this school of thought, which was later popularised in William Shirer's *The Rise and Fall of the Third Reich*.[2]

For other historians the origins of Nazism appeared to lie in the ideology and politics of particular sections of German society, allowing neither the exoneration nor the condemnation of the entire country and its history. Karl Dietrich Bracher in his monumental work, *The German Dictatorship*,[3] investigated the development of racialist-nationalist thought in nineteenth-century Europe, the ways in which the higher echelons of German society became susceptible to these ideas and how they were subsequently broadcast in Wilhelmine and Weimar society, finding a receptive audience within middle-class circles. The implications for the subsequent rise of Nazism are not hard to find and two, somewhat different, sets of explanations have been advanced by historians to explain the manifest vulnerability of Germany's (Protestant) middle classes to the appeal of Nazism. One set focuses on the victims of industrialisation: a process which caused bewilderment, disillusion and material distress among the artisans, small traders and peasants of the pre-industrial economy as they found themselves squeezed between big capital and organised labour. The other, advanced by writers such as Geoff Eley, argues that the middle classes as a whole, including the civil servants and white-collar staff who were very much part of the new, industrial age, were engulfed in a general crisis of the liberal capitalist order.[4] National Socialism was the ultimate, most extreme form of middle-class mobilisation which had antecedents in the imperialist and racist leagues of

Wilhelmine Germany.

An essential characteristic of these 'middle-class' theories is the recognition that Nazism was a 'popular' movement which derived ultimate success, at least in part, from its ability to appeal to a substantial constituency. In other words, considerable numbers of Germans had empathised with the ideological and political message which Nazism delivered. Marxist-Leninist historians found this aspect of Nazism and fascism more generally the hardest to comprehend. For them fascism constituted bourgeois capitalism's response to terminal crisis within the existing socio-economic order. National Socialism therefore arose out of capitalism, and its leaders and policies served as 'agents' through which the capitalist elites tried to reimpose order on their disintegrating world – not least through the forcible suppression of organised labour. Of course it was impossible to ignore or wish away Nazism's mass following, but for inter-war and post-war Marxist-Leninists this following consisted of a rag-bag of misled petty bourgeois and proletarians whose objective interests lay elsewhere. In the last resort Marxist-Leninist studies paid most attention to fascism (and, therefore, Nazism) as a system of rule and much less to its role as a movement of political and social mass mobilisation.

For this particular book therefore, concerned as it is with the rise of the Nazis during the Weimar era, the histories which relate Nazi ideology to the traumas of Germany's middle classes would appear inherently attractive and will be examined further when the specific role of the middle classes in the rise of Nazism is discussed. They provide an explanation for the NSDAP's successful assault on Weimar which, at least until recently, appeared to accord with the observed facts. Against this, however, other writers have tended to emphasise the class dimension rather less, instead proposing that a widespread crisis within the liberal capitalist order of inter-war Europe generated support from all quarters of society for a strong State, led by a charismatic figure, which would rise above and thereby emancipate itself from the political and social fissures which seemed to be destroying the existing order. Notable proponents of this hypothesis, starting from rather different political and analytical standpoints, have been André Gorz, Zeev Sternhell and Eugen Weber.[5] These particular writers have not been alone in noting fascism's, and Nazism's, deadly ability to combine in its ideology elements from a romantic, nostalgic, part-mythical past with demands for accelerated change and forced modernisation in society. The role of technocrats in various fascist movements and regimes is widely acknowledged, but until recently the belief that upper middle-class professionals and workers were in short supply in the Nazi movement appeared to qualify this general model to a significant degree in its specific case. Alastair Hamilton, for example, emphasised the 'petty bourgeois' basis of Nazi ideology and also its consequent poverty: 'One of the most obvious differences between the early history of the National Socialists and that of the Italian Fascists is the singular lack of appeal which National Socialism had for intellectuals'.[6]

In the past decade, however, without wishing to quibble over the poverty of Nazi ideology, our understanding of the Nazis' constituency has changed. Writers including Michael Kater and Richard Hamilton have demonstrated in different ways that professional groupings such as medics, the student population, or the Protestant upper middle-class electorate generally were strong supporters of the National Socialist movement.[7] Similarly, since Joachim Fest wrote his withering account of the Nazi elite, *The Face of the Third Reich*, concluding that his 'attempt to unravel the psychologies of the leaders of the Third Reich has laid bare, to an extent exceeding all expectation, virtually the whole range of human weaknesses, shortcomings and inadequacies',[8] views have changed somewhat. Historians have presented many of the Nazis' leaders as men of solid bourgeois provenance who could have succeeded in their personal and professional lives with or without the advent of Nazism. In other words, some were not so much the failed members of German society as relatively typical members of a society which was failing. At the other pole of society, working-class involvement in and support for the National Socialist movement has been demonstrated as significant. The working classes represented as many as four in ten party members and voters and much higher proportions than that in certain ancillary organisations such as the youth movement, the storm-troopers and the factory cells (see Documents 45–7).

The problems raised by these dicoveries are substantial. Given that Nazism rose to prominence under the shadow of the

Bolshevik Revolution, in a continent where class confrontation and social tension were often explosive, how could it have cut through this jungle of conflict to exert so widespread an appeal? Some historians have suggested that the appearance of comprehensive support belied reality. It is observed that the Nazis mobilised a substantial minority, not a majority, of Germans (although this proposition will be questioned when we examine the middle class's role in the affair) and that the large minority of German workers who backed the Nazis comprised those not involved with the organised, socialist labour movement. Instead it was those workers who subscribed to pre-industrial values or aspired to middle-class ideals who tended towards the Nazis, it is argued, thereby allowing the retention of the old middle-class model in modified form. However, the most recent work points to a substantial switch of Social Democrats to the NSDAP at the polls and even to a considerable proportion of party members who worked as wage-earners in the industrial staples sector, including metallurgy and mining. We are consequently forced to confront the question, as posed above, of how Nazism could mobilise so diverse a constituency.

II

Some historians, and contemporary observers, have remarked on the apparent cynicism of Nazi propaganda, which promised everything and anything to virtually anyone. The Nazis did indeed promise a great deal across the board, but if politics were that easy then the only obstacle to success in electoral contests would be the lack of adequate funds. Instead of perceiving this cynicism as decisive it appears necessary to identify and explore underlying unifying principles which allowed the National Socialists to reconcile these apparent programmatic contradictions and allowed their constituents to be reconciled to the same. The *völkisch* (ethnic populist) dimension of Nazi ideology appears crucial in this regard and therefore deserves careful examination, particularly in contemporary Europe where both dangerous and potentially attractive examples of this phenomenon are thriving. The precise character of German *völkisch* thought is best examined at some length within its historical context, but it presumed that all Germans shared a common ethnicity, culture and set of values which stemmed from a glorious (part-mythologised) history. These common bonds were held to be far more important than any divisions, social or otherwise, within the German nation and, furthermore, were held to demonstrate the innate superiority of Germandom over its neighbours, or any other people including, tragically, Germany's Jewish minority. Implicitly at least, *völkisch* thought provided the legitimation for an expansionist foreign policy and for the suppression of political pluralism at home.

In *The German Dictatorship* Bracher acknowledged the importance of *völkisch* ideology for Nazism, considered its aggressive sense of cultural mission and noted its claim that nationhood based on shared values rooted in a common history (often viewed romantically and nostalgically) counted for more than the intellectual artifice of the (French) revolutionary nation State. The *völkisch* reverence for the strong State was also very apparent, but Bracher passes relatively briefly over the manifest contrast between this ideal and the reality of the German situation before 1866 or 1870.[9]

Edmond Vermeil, however, emphasised these particular conflicts and tensions which have bedevilled Germany throughout its history. The medieval Holy Roman Empire witnessed the beginnings of a decline in central, imperial power, but, as this decline subsequently accelerated, 'By the simple play of compensation, culture gained in cohesion and extension at the times when territorial fragmentation condemned the nation to political impotence'.[10] As Friedrich von Schiller was to comment in 1804: 'The German Empire and the German nation are two different things. The glory of the Germans has never been based upon the power of its princes.'[11] French annexation of imperial territories over centuries culminated in direct Napoleonic control of lands well to the east of the Rhine, leaving the nation's physical weakness to stand in stark contrast with the cohesiveness and universal validity of German culture. If, during the Cold War era, Federal Germany quickly developed as a strong State devoid of a national identity or mission, early nineteenth-century Germany possessed a powerful national culture in search of a commensurately strong State.

With the proclamation of the German Empire in January 1871, German power again became the potentially decisive factor on the European continent after a hiatus of many hundreds of years. However, the Prusso-German Reich left many millions of Germans outwith its boundaries (notably in the multi-national Habsburg Empire) and failed to develop a sustainable, stable relationship with France or to maintain one with Russia. The German national question remained acute and even intensified as the Habsburg Empire drifted into crisis during the early 1900s and the Wilhelmine Reich's own aggressive foreign policy provoked powerful reactions among its neighbours. Germany's defeat in the ensuing war threw the contrast between the nation's potential and actual strength into particularly stark relief. The Weimar Republic was too greatly weakened and hamstrung by the Paris Peace Settlement to realise the aspirations of Germans within and beyond its frontiers, but the previous grandeur of the Empire and the tantalising possibilities presented by the Treaty of Brest-Litovsk in March 1918 combined to convince many Germans that their country was truly a Sampson in chains. The presence of foreign troops on their soil and the involvement of foreign commissioners in the innermost workings of the economy, the detachment of German-speaking territories from the Republic and the stringent disarmament provisions reinforced the conviction that the natural order of things had been inverted in grotesque and unjust fashion.

What went unsaid by and large was that the willingness of Germany's government to risk war in 1914 and the radical annexationist wartime policies supported by the country's elites contributed in handsome measure to this catastrophe. Indeed the Treaty of Versailles was less damaging to Germany than Brest-Litovsk had been to the Soviet Union, but Germany's elites either denied culpability or silently awaited an opportunity to overthrow the Republic and the Paris Peace Settlement. Writing during the 1960s, Fritz Fischer was the first major post-war historian to pursue this line of argument and also to emphasise the continuities between the foreign policies of the Wilhelmine Empire, the Weimar Republic and the Third Reich.[12] Subsequently a generation of German historians of the centre-left has taken the matter further, investigating the Wilhelmine establishment's ability to rally popular support around its radical and aggressive foreign policy (*Weltpolitik*). The elites' behaviour, therefore, has understandably diverted some historians' attention away from the issue of popular nationalism. The broad middle classes were seen as the primary targets of elitist appeals, although the English historians David Blackbourn and Geoff Eley suggested that the role of the middle classes was not so passive. Whilst Fischer and his close supporters maintained that *Weltpolitik* was devised and pursued by the Prusso-German aristocracy to enlist support for the country's autocratic, monarchist system of government, Eley and Blackbourn argued that the same nationalism emanated in large measure from the aspirations and concerns of the middle classes themselves and that leading proponents of *Weltpolitik*, such as Admiral von Tirpitz, consciously sought by means of naval and colonial expansion to favour the modern, dynamic elements in German society.[13]

Eley in particular took the argument further by proposing that this populist nationalism was subsequently to constitute an important element in emergent fascism, under which heading he included Nazism. Implicitly at least, his analysis indicated the context within which *völkisch* ideology would operate after the Great War. He was little concerned with its possible resonance in working-class circles, but proposed that populist nationalism could fuse together traditional and modern, very disparate middle-class interests.[14] For this insight he received little thanks from some social democratic German colleagues who appeared to fear that his case rather let the Empire's elites off the hook.

Historians such as Hans Mommsen and Hans-Ulrich Wehler did investigate dimensions of the relationship between labour and the national question, but neither suggested that significant numbers of workers could have been embraced by a *völkisch* movement.[15] When Roger Fletcher showed that some pre-1914 socialist intellectuals were attracted by the notion of a 'classless folk community (*Volksgemeinschaft*), in which a culturally-defined nationality principle would form the main criterion of membership',[16] his critics replied that such thinking was restricted to a relatively narrow circle associated with the journal *Sozialistische Monatshefte* which was the focus of his investigations.

All in all, *völkisch* nationalism has been recognised as a factor contributing to the rise of Nazism, albeit generally in the context of middle-class politics. Some historians, such as Jeremy Noakes, have accorded it a major role,[17] but most recent and contemporary studies have not paid an inordinate amount of attention to it. Perhaps this has been inevitable. It is a commonplace that historical writing reflects the time and locus of its authorship as much as it investigates its subject. In *The Nazi Dictatorship* Ian Kershaw demonstrates convincingly, if implicitly, how true this has been of recent writing in the former East and West Germanies.[18] Neither entity, built up as a superpower client State on the wreckage of the old Reich, was fertile ground for a historiography which gave great prominence to the role of national sentiment in history. There were other fish to fry. This was all the more so since the Third Reich appeared to represent the culmination of German nationalism and the now-silent concentration camps its epitaph. Only in the past few years has the latent power of national feeling been impressed on mainstream West European thinking by events in Central and Eastern Europe.

In the former communist states of Eastern Europe this newly virulent nationalism has assumed grotesque and violent forms which are unmistakably *völkisch* in tone and content. This is not entirely surprising, for many parts of Eastern Europe lack a historic burgher class and the accompanying civic institutions and consciousness which were an essential prerequisite for the development of liberal-revolutionary nationalism in late eighteenth- or nineteenth-century Western Europe or eighteenth-century North America. German *völkisch* nationalism cannot, however, be compared with current East European forms, at least in terms of its origins. Germany had seen the growth during the middle ages of the Hanseatic towns and the imperial city States, within which a confident burgher class thrived, leading the nineteenth-century thinker, Otto von Gierke, to see this civic development as a vital root of modern German statehood.[19] Furthermore, as Michael Hughes has demonstrated, the internal arrangements of the later Holy Roman Empire provided substantial provincial, corporative and individual liberties under the aegis of imperial law. As a result the intellectual climate in late eighteenth-century Germany was by no means hostile to the Empire as such.[20] In foreign affairs, however, things were different, and here it might be apposite to reiterate the picture painted of pre-unification Germany by Vermeil, where national sentiment was encouraged to develop on *völkisch* lines not for want of a robust civil society, but for the want of an unambiguous German statehood. The most meaningful definition of Germanness was cultural and, perhaps, historic, although *völkisch* thinkers lauded the concept of the strong State as a means to resolve the paradox between Germany's cultural virility and political weakness. The Bismarckian and Wilhelmine Reich brought a resolution of this problem tantalisingly close, but failed, and the State ultimately teetered on the brink of disintegration in 1918. The victorious Allies allowed the Weimar Republic to retain most of the Empire's territory and economic potential, but to Germans in Europe it appeared yet again that they were parcelled out between a variety of States and were left at the beck and call of their adversaries.

German political parties responded to this mood at the war's end, adopting and adapting the concept of *Volksgemeinschaft* (popular ethnic community). This had become the watchword of various groups who had sought, in Gunther Mai's words, 'to reconcile national and social integration or "liberation" respectively'.[21] The German Conservative Party renamed itself the German National People's Party (DNVP) and the National Liberal Party became the German People's Party (DVP). The inclusion of the adjective 'People's' was not intended to mollify specifically working-class aspirations, but instead to appeal to notions of *völkisch* solidarity. These concepts were also embraced by the Catholic Centre Party and the Catholic unions were the first to combine the notions of 'national-socialism' and *Volksgemeinschaft* in 1920. The Marxist parties themselves, however, were not untouched by the intense *völkisch* nationalism of the post-war years. The Communist Party wrestled with the challenge posed by working-class *völkisch* sentiment, sometimes appealing to it, sometimes decrying it and sometimes sinking into ideological confusion as different Communist leaders adopted contrasting stances on this issue. The Social Democrats, as the main representatives of organised labour in Weimar Germany, also appeared to ascribe legitimacy to *völkisch* nationalism in their 1921 Görlitz Programme, although this stance was reversed and class politics again stressed in the 1925 Heidelberg Programme.

Although these and other parties subscribed to or flirted with *völkisch* ideals, all were singularly ill equipped to mobilise a mass constituency under the *völkisch* banner. They were direct descendants of parties which had sat in the near-toothless imperial Reichstag, lobbying for their particular constituents and making political deals on their behalf, but never countenancing the prospect of executive power or pursuing national interests. Under Bismarck's constitution such matters were left to the aristocratic ministers appointed by the Emperor, leading Max Weber in 1917 to bemoan the immaturity of Germany's political parties.[22] The SPD had broader aspirations, but these depended on the working-class electorate becoming numerically predominant and then voting more or less *en bloc* for Social Democracy. Neither was to happen. At the end of the day a great deal of political space was left unfilled in the new Republic and remained so until the 1930 elections. Bracher observes that this vacuum was filled on the institutional level through reliance on presidential authority (issuing emergency decrees and sanctioning periods of minority government),[23] but popular mobilisation under one banner, either for or against the Republic, was conspicuous by its absence. There were many non-party organisations which espoused *völkisch* ideals from the outset, but all were either paramilitary leagues or closed, even elitist, conspiratorial organisations which neither sought nor could have obtained broad electoral support. The National Socialists stepped into and ultimately filled this void, but were also, in ideological terms, a product of it.

III

The main focus and location of *völkisch* agitation shifted decisively between the early and late nineteenth century. At the beginning *völkisch* leaders, such as Friedrich Jahn, had regarded Napoleonic France as the main threat to German territorial, institutional, cultural and ethical integrity; the Slavonic, Russian Empire was a potential or actual friend. Hopes of a liaison with Russia were never entirely abandoned by *völkisch* and nationalist thinkers, but by the end of the nineteenth century fears focused more on the perceived threat posed by the numerical strength of their Slavonic neighbours and by a Slavonic cultural and political revival. Within Germany itself writers such as Paul de Lagarde and Houston Stewart Chamberlain posited a racialist nationalism which pitted the superior, Germanic peoples against their Slavonic and Latin neighbours – and against an alleged 'enemy within', the Jews. Organisations such as the Pan German League lobbied for a vigorous expansionist policy, overseas but also in Eastern Europe, and had the ear of some senior government officials for their unashamedly racialist programme. Linkages between this *fin de siècle* thinking and subsequent Nazi ideology are evident and have often been remarked upon by historians.

In the Austrian Habsburg lands tensions between German and Slav were very much greater as a numerically inferior, but socio-economically and politically dominant German population began to feel threatened by the majority Slav population. The conflict was focused in the historic Czech lands of Bohemia, Moravia and Austrian Silesia, a region which had witnessed substantial German colonisation in preceding centuries, colonists whose assumptions of cultural and social superiority were reinforced by the presence of a German-speaking, Habsburg administrative and military elite. The national struggle in the Czech lands therefore became a social struggle – between (German) employers and (Czech) employees, (German) skilled workers and (Czech) labourers, and between Germans and Czechs for jobs in the civil service and on the railways. Disputes flared over the language of education, the use of Czech in the public service and the settlement of Czech labourers in German-speaking industrial regions. These conflicts soon found an echo in political life. German nationalists created Defence Leagues (*Schutzvereine*) to safeguard that which, given their numerical inferiority, the ballot box might not. The national issue also led to the birth of new political movements which were defined both by their social constituency and their Germanness, and ultimately to the birth of new parties. The German Workers' Party, founded in 1904, and the German Agrarians (1905) both represented their specific constituencies, but also collaborated with other nationalist groups on a formal basis. Most German-speaking workers in the Czech lands continued to vote Social Democrat right up to the Great War but, as Elizabeth Wiskemann noted, the German Workers' Party represented the first example of working-class opposition to the Social Democrats in the name of ethnic solidarity.[24]

Anti-Semitism, as exemplified by the politics of Georg von Schönerer among others, also had a significant following in the

Austrian lands and certainly a far greater popular resonance than within the German Empire itself (see Document 6). It is, therefore, no accident that the post-1918 National Socialists were located in Bohemia-Moravia, Austria and across the border in Bavaria where the authorities indulged their activities. However, the national crisis which swept Germany following defeat and harsh peace conditions gave National Socialism a resonance throughout the country, providing a context within which it and a whole rag-bag of *völkisch*, imperialist and nationalist ideals seemed to make sense and seemed to explain the nation's predicament more convincingly than other ideologies could. National Socialist ideology did not amount to much in itself, for it borrowed and stole from elsewhere as appropriate. In as far as certain Weimar academics posited a German cultural mission in Eastern Europe and a causal relationship between ethnicity (or even race) and the history of the East, Nazism could not even claim to have developed an updated *völkisch* nationalism in the Weimar era. Its biological, deterministic racialism did admittedly represent a significant innovation in terms of its radicalism and coherence, even if the practical consequences of this racialism had to await the establishment of the Nazi state; but historians have remarked on the poverty of Nazi ideology and on its wafer-thin theoretical foundations to the point where some have suggested that it was merely an accumulation of negative objectives and feelings (an 'anti' movement). This, however, underestimates the extent and intensity of *völkisch* sentiment in Weimar Germany and the degree to which the *völkisch* 'myth' lent a coherence and purpose to the Nazi programme which it would otherwise have entirely lacked.

The importance of the mobilising myth as a trigger to revolutionary action was remarked upon in 1908 by Georges Sorel in his seminal work *Reflections on Violence*. He concluded that there was little value in abstract theorisation, in part because of humanity's inability to predict the future with any great accuracy, but also because complex philosophies of politics, history or economics are a poor spur to revolutionary passion and commitment. In place of this, Sorel posited a myth which could be perceived by potential revolutionaries as a simplified but intuitively meaningful allegory of a much more complex reality:

Those myths which enclose with them all the strongest inclinations of a people, of a party or of a class, inclinations which recur to the mind with the insistence of instincts in all circumstances of life; and which give an aspect of complete reality to the hopes of immediate action by which, more easily than by any other method, men can reform their desires passions and mental activity.[25]

For Sorel as an anarcho-syndicalist, the myth of the general strike appeared all important, serving as the most effective allegorical encapsulation of socialist sentiment and revolutionary struggle. In the hour and aftermath of defeat, however, the German nation was particularly receptive to the *völkisch* myth.

This *völkisch* myth was lent far greater resonance and a contemporary, concrete form in the shape of the *Frontgemeinschaft*, or front-line community. This particular interpretation of wartime experience claimed that the universal dangers and general suffering of the wartime trenches had united soldiers from every background in a common struggle against the enemy. This solidarity was contrasted with the conflict-laden nature of domestic parliamentary politics where fellow Germans fought for their individual corner rather than for the greater national good (see Document 17). Veterans' associations, such as the Stahlhelm which eventually attracted 500,000 members, combined advocacy of the front-line community with demands for the restoration of the monarchy. More sinister were the *Freikorps* (Volunteer Corps), within which a combination of military veterans and youth of the immediate post-war generation fought to put down the radical left on government orders in 1919, subsequently fought Polish irregular forces in Upper Silesia, but soon turned to attacking the Republic and individual republican politicians who were construed as the 'enemy within'. Many *Freikorps* leaders subsequently found their way into the leadership cadre of Hitler's storm-troopers. Both the *Freikorps* and the Stahlhelm found that their militant espousal of *völkisch* solidarity had a broad social appeal, with university students, middle-class citizens and farm and factory workers rubbing shoulders within these organisations. The war experience had imparted not only a sense of common cause, but also a pronounced consciousness of hierarchy, of giving orders and of obeying. This replaced civil class barriers by a military ethos which many male Germans appeared to find preferable to civilian stratification. Equally striking was the emulation of militarist ideals across a broad swathe of the political spectrum. That the Communists should have formed a paramilitary arm (in 1924) is not entirely surprising, but if imitation is indeed the sincerest form of flattery, the name given to it – the Red Front-Line Fighters' League – is noteworthy. However, the republican, pro-parliamentary parties – SPD, Centre and DDP – were so concerned by the attraction of the *völkisch*, militarist ethos for male German youth that they too formed a paramilitary league in 1924, the Reichsbanner (National Flag) Black Red Gold. Of course these were the republican, not the imperial, colours, but the espousal of paramilitary politics and the appeal to national sentiment by the parliamentarian parties was at best an admission that in this vital respect the democratic pass had already been sold.

None of the anti-republican leagues, however, were equipped to overthrow the constitution. Left- and right-wingers had resorted to various coup and *Putsch* attempts during the early 1920s, but the left was invariably crushed by the monarchist armed forces and the right defeated either by resolute trade union action (Kapp *Putsch*, 1920) or by the unwillingness of senior army commanders to tolerate the violent overthrow of the constitution, despite their personal sympathy for elements of the *völkisch* programme. The leagues were unable or unwilling to enter the electoral fray, for that was the province of the despised party politicians, but in this regard the National Socialist movement differed. It may have suffered a dearth of original ideological insights, but Hitler's willingness to carry the *völkisch* struggle into Parliament, the heartland of his political foes, gave it long-term prospects which other such movements lacked. Until the Munich *Putsch* of November 1923, Hitler's political strategy had been dominated by his association with the Bavarian paramilitary milieu of which the SA of the NSDAP was an integral part. The failure of the *Putsch*, however, moved him to accord unquestioned primacy to the Nazi Party and the parliamentary struggle within the movement; the Republic was to be destroyed through the ballot box.

IV

Squaring the circle between an avowed hostility to the Republican order and a simultaneous willingness more or less to play the game by its rules was not straightforward. The authorities were deeply suspicious of the NSDAP, monitored its activities and restricted Hitler's right to speak in public; only from September 1928 was he allowed to address meetings in Social Democratic Prussia. The problems within his own movement were possibly even greater. His paramilitary leaders were never comfortable with the 'legality' policy, for it downgraded their own role and appeared to taint National Socialism with the self-seeking, venal attitudes which they associated with party politics. Relations between the SA and the Party Organisation (PO) were sometimes very strained indeed.

In defence of his stand Hitler emphasised from the outset that unlike the other parties, which represented particular sectional interests, the NSDAP reflected and projected the general, popular will (see Documents 10, 14, 15). The future National Socialist State would accordingly be just that, a one-party State which furthered the interests and aspirations of the entire *völkisch* community. His personal role within the movement carried this argument further, for in *Mein Kampf* he decried both pluralistic political systems and executive decision-making within any context on a collegiate basis. The free play of ideas was only beneficial up to the point where the strongest had triumphed, and competition between individual leaders only acceptable until a natural, supreme leader had emerged (see Document 34). Hitler, of course, saw himself in this role and in this regard introduced an element into National Socialist ideology which, as Francis Carsten observes, had been lacking in the early Nazi parties of Central Europe, where a more democratic and open style of leadership had prevailed.[26] Hitler therefore claimed to be the embodiment of a stridently racialist *völkisch* popular will, and that he, to quote another (altogether more distinguished) twentieth-century grandee 'belonged to no one' and yet, as the self-appointed saviour of his people, belonged 'to everyone'. No other individual Weimar party leader could have made or would have made this claim (see Document 35).

This vision of power and politics was deeply at variance with the reality of public life in twentieth-century North-western Europe. Max Weber had observed that modern capitalist society was becoming increasingly bureaucratised and that rules, regulations and routine were displacing personal power and individual responsibility. More recently André Gorz remarked pithily that 'It's no longer people who have power; it's the positions of power which have their people', and that the State is a 'mechanism of power to which every citizen is subordinated and which, at the same time, denies personal power to everyone'.[27] However, at least during their period as opposition movements, fascism and Nazism have been perceived by many writers as a rebellion against this state of affairs. Individual citizens are only partly willing to admit or to perceive that functional routine plays a disproportionate part in modern society. Although they may complain about 'the system' – a complaint the Nazis took up and addressed with vigour – they are equally likely to seek demons and saviours in times of profound national and social crisis. The republican parties, such as the Social Democrats, were very much bound up in the functionalist routine of the Weimar State, but Hitler was able to offer himself as the potential saviour of Germany and its people. His demons resembled those of the mainstream, anti-republican right, but his biological racialism and his conviction that this was in accordance with the natural laws of history allowed him to construct a political allegory with which a broad cross-section of the German population could empathise. And most Germans did take Hitler's message to be allegorical rather than literal, with even some German Jews reluctant to accept that his anti-Semitism might ultimately be played out in practice. He had provided a mobilising myth which emphasised the sameness of all Germans precisely at a time when a divided, fragmented society was looking for such an escape from crisis. The Jews were taken to symbolise unnatural, alien forces which had disrupted natural social harmony, although of course Hitler's own view of the Jews' role in Germany's disaster was far more literal (see Documents 7, 8, 19).

Virtually all aspects of National Socialist ideology either drew on precedent or mirrored aspects of contemporary German thinking and concerns. However, this same ideology took care to adopt and adapt thinking and to address issues which focused on the perceived humiliation and suppression of a potentially dominant nation. The adjective 'socialist' within the NSDAP's title was meant sincerely, but only in irrevocable tandem with the adjective 'national' (see Documents 9, 10, 14, 18). It was the socialism of a thwarted ruling people (*Herrenvolk*) rather than that of the chronically underprivileged and oppressed seeking justice and equal rights. Hitler, as the charismatic leader of Germany, aimed to effect the salvation of his people not just from its external enemies, but also at their expense (see Documents 11, 13). This form of socialism could appeal across class barriers with far greater ease than could Marxist socialism, which posed uncomfortable dilemmas for middle-class citizens. Similarly, Nazi nationalism did not necessarily have the same negative connotations for the working classes as did bourgeois, let alone Wilhelmine, nationalism. Furthermore, Hitler's personal political strategy and his success in legitimising it ideologically gave the National Socialists a practical route, through Parliament, towards the realisation of their aims. However, ideology alone was not to bring Hitler to power. The organisational structure of the National Socialist movement, its political programme and the environment, political and socio-economic, within which it operated were all to be crucial.

Notes

1   A. J. P. Taylor, *The Course of German History. A Survey of the Development of Germany since 1815*, London, 1945, p. 114.

2   William L. Shirer, *The Rise and Fall of the Third Reich*, New York, London, 1960.

3   Karl Dietrich Bracher, *The German Dictatorship. The Origins, Structure and Effects of National Socialism*, trans. J. Steinberg, London, 1973, ch. 1.

4   Geoff Eley, *From Unification to Nazism. Reinterpreting the German Past*, Winchester, Mass. and London, 1986, chs. 9 and 10.

5   André Gorz, *Farewell to the Working Class. An Essay on Post-Industrial Socialism*, trans. M. Sonenscher, London, 1982, ch. 5. Zeev Sternhell, 'Fascist Ideology', in Walter Laqueur (ed.), *Fascism: A Reader's Guide: Analyses, Interpretations, Bibliography*, London, 1976, ch. 9. Eugen Weber, 'Revolution? Counter-revolution? What Revolution?', in Laqueur, *Fascism*, ch. 12.

6   Alastair Hamilton, *The Appeal of Fascism. A Study of Intellectuals and Fascism 1919–1945*, New York, 1971, pp. 102–3.

7 Michael J. Kater, *Doctors under Hitler*, Chapel Hill, London, 1989; *The Nazi Party. A Social Profile of Members and Leaders, 1919–1945*, London, 1983, esp. pp. 44–50, 62–71. Richard F. Hamilton, *Who Voted for Hitler?*, Princeton, NJ, 1982.

8 Joachim C. Fest, *The Face of the Third Reich*, trans. M. Bullock, London, 1972, p. 435.

9 Bracher, *German Dictatorship*, pp. 20–52.

10 Edmond Vermeil, *Germany's Three Reichs. Their History and Culture*, trans. E. W. Dickes, London, 1945, p. 53.

11 Quoted in Michael Hughes, 'Fiat justitia, pereat Germania? The imperial supreme jurisdiction and imperial reform in the later Holy Roman Empire', in John Breuilly (ed.), *The State of Germany. The national idea in the making, unmaking and remaking of a modern nation state*, London, New York, 1992, p. 31.

12 Fritz Fischer, *Germany's Aims in the First World War*, London, 1967; *War of Illusions*, London, 1973; *From Kaiserreich to Third Reich: Elements of Continuity in German History 1871–1945*, trans. R. Fletcher, London, Boston, Sydney, 1986.

13 David Blackbourn and Geoff Eley, *The Peculiarities of German History. Bourgeois Society and Politics in Nineteenth-Century Germany*, Oxford, New York, 1984.

14 Geoff Eley, *Reshaping the German Right. Radical Nationalism and Political Change after Bismarck*, New Haven, London, 1980.

15 Hans Mommsen, *Arbeiterbewegung und Nationale Frage. Aufgewählte Aufsätze*, Göttingen, 1979. Hans-Ulrich Wehler, *Sozialdemokratie und Nationalstaat. Nationalitätenfragen in Deutschland 1840–1914*, Göttingen, 1971.

16 Roger Fletcher, 'Revisionism and Wilhelmine Imperialism', *Journal of Contemporary History*, 23, 1988, p. 357; *Revisionism and Empire: Socialist Imperialism in Germany 1897–1914*, London, 1984.

17 Jeremy Noakes, *The Nazi Party in Lower Saxony 1921–1933*, Oxford, 1971.

18 Ian Kershaw, *The Nazi Dictatorship. Problems and Perspectives of Interpretation*, London, 1985, ch. 1.

19 Antony Black (ed.), *Community in Historical Perspective. A translation of selections from Das deutsche Genossenschaftsrecht by Otto von Gierke*, trans. M. Fischer, Cambridge, New York, 1990, esp. ch. 6.

20 Hughes, 'Fiat justitia'.

21 Gunther Mai, 'National Socialist Factory Cell Organisation and German Labour Front . . .', in Conan Fischer (ed.), *Weimar, the Working Classes and the Rise of National Socialism*, Oxford, 1995, forthcoming.

22 Quoted in Bracher, *German Dictatorship*, p. 106.

23 *Ibid.*, pp. 216–27. See also Karl Dietrich Bracher, 'Democracy and the Power Vacuum: The Problem of the Party State during the Disintegration of the Weimar Republic', in Volker R. Berghahn and Martin Kitchen (eds.), *Germany in the Age of Total War*, London, Totowa, NJ, 1981.

24 Elizabeth Wiskemann, *Czechs and Germans. A Study of the Struggle in the Historic Provinces of Bohemia and Moravia*, 2nd edn., London, New York, 1967, p. 65.

25 'Georges Sorel', in J. S. McClelland (ed.), *The French Right from de Maistre to Maurras*, London, 1970, p. 127.

26 Francis Carsten, *Fascist Movements in Austria. From Schönerer to Hitler*, London, 1977, pp. 74–5.

27 Gorz, *Farewell*, p. 57.

3

National Socialist policy and propaganda

National Socialist ideology and propaganda are often regarded as two sides of the same coin and justifiably so. It is through propaganda, of course, that many parties seek to disseminate their ideology, but the dynamism and militaristic values of Nazism resulted in its propaganda often serving as the message itself. SA marches and concerts, mass rallies and sporting exhibitions were very much cases in point. If ideology and propaganda have been subjected to widespread scrutiny, much less has been written explicitly on National Socialist policy before 1933. In some cases ideology alone has been regarded as the Nazi message, with policies such as Gregor Strasser's job creation programme of 1932 left entirely out of the equation. In others the issue is merely semantic. Thus Barbara Miller Lane's and Leila Rupp's documentation of pre-1933 Nazi ideology includes programmatic statements which might equally be regarded as policy proposals, as well as policies on issues such as agriculture and employment.[1]

As seen previously, National Socialist ideology was derivative and diffuse, but through its encapsulation of a powerful allegorical, mythologised vision of the condition and fate of the German nation it acquired a certain coherence and resonance. Yet however compelling or attractive this ideology might have been, and however effective its projection through propaganda campaigns, the NSDAP also had to indicate the policies it would pursue once in power if it wished to be more than a fringe, protest party.

The infant German Workers' Party (DAP) published a set of 'Guidelines' in January 1919 which anticipated parts of the NSDAP's Programme, or 'Twenty-Five Points'. The 'Guidelines', however, were briefer and were concerned with a narrower range of issues: the future of the skilled working classes, the Jewish question and the legacy of war and defeat. The best prospects for skilled workers were seen to lie in social consensus; their material betterment would be achieved through profit sharing within co-operatives and via agreements with foreign trade unions to prevent competing economies undercutting each other's wage levels. The 'Guidelines' had relatively little to say on foreign policy, but advocated retrospective taxation of all high wartime incomes (above 10,000RM per annum) to meet the costs of the war. They also warned against the nationalisation of industry since State-owned companies might have been confiscated as reparations by the victor powers. The Jews were vilified as wealthy, lazy manipulators who constituted an undesirable alien presence in German society, not least because they put their personal interests, or those of foreign powers, above German interests. The 'Guidelines' indicated that Jews would be excluded from public life.

In addition to this more or less official programme, individual writers such as Dietrich Eckart, Alfred Rosenberg and Gottfried Feder gave indications of the policies a National Socialist government might pursue. In 1918 Feder, who was to play a significant part in the formulation of the 'Twenty-Five Points' drafted his 'Manifesto for Breaking the Bondage of Interest', which was published in mid-1919. It included a series of proposals which have been viewed by Lane and Rupp as advocating 'a thoroughgoing state socialism':[2] the nationalisation of banks, a major state role in transport, utilities and natural resources, the use of monetary policy to influence price and wage levels, the confiscation of excess profits to the benefit of welfare programmes, and state participation in the urban land and property markets. Above all of this, however, Feder distinguished between 'industrial' and 'loan' capital, the latter parasitical, dominant and growing ever more so through the charging, compounding and re-charging of interest. This 'bondage of interest', Feder argued, was responsible for division and strife within society and he therefore advocated converting interest-bearing debt to non-interest-bearing legal tender with money eventually serving only as 'an exchange for labour'.

Eckart shared Feder's aversion to 'loan' capital, but imbued it with a Jewish character which reflected a virulent anti-Semitism, qualified only by the contention that the creativity and dynamism contained in Jewish values made them a necessary evil (see Documents 7, 8). In *Mein Kampf*, of course, Hitler was to deny even this concession. Rosenberg's anti-Semitism added the Bolshevik Revolution to the litany of alleged Jewish crimes and although there may have been an element of cynical opportunism in his anti-Semitic writings he had in effect created the 'conspiracy of Jewish Bolsheviks and Jewish bankers closing in on Germany'.[3]

This range of ideas combined with those of Hitler to produce the 'Twenty-Five Points' of the NSDAP. Drafted in early 1920, but only published in a full definitive version in 1923, these Points provided a broader statement of intent than that within the DAP's 'Guidelines'. Feder's ideas on State intervention in the economy, collectivism and the redistribution of wealth were carried over into Points 9 to 14, while Point 18, which promised the death sentence to 'usurers' and 'profiteers' among others, satisfied his antipathy to interest-bearing loans. The NSDAP's anti-Semitic intentions were made plain in Points 4 to 8 and Point 24, which in sum promised the exclusion of Jews from public life, the removal of their citizenship rights and, if needs be, their expulsion from Germany. Hitler's foreign policy aspirations were reflected in Points 1 to 3, which advocated the overthrow of the Paris Peace Settlement, the union of all ethnic Germans in a single State and the acquisition of additional territory for settlement. Further Points promised wide-ranging reforms including enhanced welfare, health and educational opportunities, a people's army, the scrapping of the Civil Code in favour of Germanic common law, extensive control over the press and publishing and the creation of a centralised, corporate State. All in all, ethnic Germans were being invited to trade their individual freedom for material security and national greatness at the expense of allegedly non-ethnic Germans within the country and at the expense of Germany's neighbours (see Document 19).

The broad parameters of this programme were never to be substantially challenged from within the party. However, the

'Twenty-Five Points' provided no clear idea of how its objectives would be fulfilled, still less any indication of the impact its vague prescriptions would have on the day-to-day lives of German voters. Considerably more detail was provided by a 'Comprehensive Programme of National Socialism' which was drafted by the north German Strasser group during the winter of 1925–26. Its prescriptions for wide areas of foreign and domestic policy have provided valuable insights into the thinking of leading National Socialists during the mid-1920s; a corporatist constitution, considerable public involvement in the economy and a pre-eminent role for Germany in Europe were all confirmed.

The motivation of its authors sounds radical. Gregor Strasser emphasised that the 'Programme' was to serve as the basis for a 'Second Revolution'; 'to make up for the one which failed [1918] because of the cowardice and inability of its leaders and because of the doctrinal limitations of Marxist theory'.[4] Otto Strasser and Joseph Goebbels interpreted Stalinism as a Russian form of National Socialism and therefore postulated a German foreign policy conducted in alliance with, rather than against, the Soviet Union. However, the 'Programme's' considerable detail accorded by and large with the spirit of the 'Twenty-Five Points', and in any case it remained merely a draft. At a meeting of National Socialist leaders in Bamberg in February 1926 Hitler prevailed upon its authors to drop their proposals. He does not seem to have objected to them as such, but declared their timing to be inopportune. Furthermore, he did not wish his role as Führer and thus as the personal embodiment of Nazism to be jeopardised by the production of detailed party programmes. The generalities of the 'Twenty-Five Points' served him and, he argued, the party very well.

Although the 'Points' were declared to be immutable, the phrasing of Point 17 became somewhat embarrassing to the party by 1928. During that year the NSDAP was enjoying its first successes in the Protestant countryside, prompting opponents to draw attention to this part of the Nazi programme, which reserved for the State the right to expropriate agricultural land. Hitler had no wish in any case to collectivise farming land and in a note of clarification to Point 17 declared in April that it was directed primarily against Jewish speculators.

The property rights of peasants and farmers appeared safe, but this was not the NSDAP's final word on rural policy. In March 1930 the *Völkischer Beobachter* published an 'Official Statement on Farmers and Agriculture'. This blended straightforward concessions to the farming community with conditions and restrictions which made it plain that the NSDAP was not just another agrarian party. Germany's taxation and tariff policies were to be revised in favour of the agricultural sector, credit was to be cheap and readily available to farmers, and a range of inputs including machinery, fertilizers and power were to be provided more cheaply through State or other corporate agencies. However, in a text laced with implicit and explicit anti-Semitism, it was made plain that a strong farming sector served wider economic, racial and military objectives: 'We . . . see in the farmers the main bearers of a healthy *völkisch* heredity, the fountain of youth and the people, and the backbone of military power'.[5] Self-sufficiency in foodstuffs was also deemed to provide an escape from 'bondage by debt to international high finance', since Germany would no longer have to borrow to pay for food imports.

Despite Hitler's 1928 note of clarification, this instrumentalist view of the farming population led the NSDAP to reiterate demands for the curtailment of property rights on land which had been advocated by some German legal theorists for decades. Farmers would retain title, but an avowedly 'German' land law would make ownership conditional on collective needs being met and a law of entailment would regulate rights of disposal and inheritance. Finally, the 'Statement' emphasised the need for farm labour also to benefit from the resulting prosperity and reminded farmers that their emancipation could only occur as part of a general 'political liberation' of the German people 'of every occupation and rank' (see Document 20).[6] This point was reiterated by Walther Darré, head of the NSDAP's Agricultural Affairs Bureau, in April 1931. Attempts by any single occupational group to improve its lot in isolation were dismissed by the Statement as 'madness' and thus, in contrast to the agrarian parties, the NSDAP presented itself here as the party of town and country, of national solidarity and renewal (see Document 21).

As will be seen, this agricultural programme was harnessed by Darré in a bid to mobilise the rural population behind the NSDAP, but parallel to it was a job creation programme which constituted a major part of Nazi economic policy during the July

1932 election campaign. Gregor Strasser was most closely associated with this element of policy and had spoken in the
Reichstag in October 1930 to propose a compulsory labour service
and deficit-funded public works as means of eradicating unemployment. He differed strikingly from Hitler and most leading
Nazis in pursuing a consensual approach to day-to-day politics,
and in spring 1932 members of his Political Economy Department
participated in the Study Society for Systems of Finance and
Credit. This body was founded by the industrialist Heinrich
Dräger and the finance expert Rudolf Dalberg and was influenced
by the thinking of Silvio Gesells and the experience of the wartime economy in its efforts to prescribe a solution to the unemployment crisis. Its membership included prominent trade union
leaders such as Vladimir Woytinski and Fritz Tarnow (who were
involved in the Social Democratic Unions' own job creation
plans) as well as a number of leading industrialists. Among the
Nazis was Fritz Reinhardt, who was to lend his name to the Nazi
government's recovery programme of early 1933. As Udo
Kissenkoetter remarks, this Society included the key elements
from which General von Schleicher was to seek to form a broadly
based coalition government in December 1932.[7]

In the immediate term, however, the Society provided Strasser
with many of the fundamentals of his 'Work and Bread' programme (see Document 22). He readily acknowledged Hitler's
role as the embodiment of the National Socialist ethos, but saw
himself as the formulator of practical policy. In May 1932 he
addressed the Reichstag in terms which were corporatist and
solidarist, rather than libertarian, on the need to create new jobs.
Priority had to be given to 'work and achievement' rather than to
'money, profit and dividends', and property had to be 'an
honourable return for honest work' rather than the outcome of
speculative adventures in the international economy.[8] Like Feder
before him he was unwittingly anticipating the infamous slogan
'Labour liberates' (*Arbeit macht frei*), above the gates of Auschwitz
concentration camp.

With natural resources and work seen as the origins of capital
everyone was to be guaranteed employment, but would simultaneously be bound by a universal obligation to work. New jobs
would be created on the land and through a rural housing programme designed to resettle city dwellers. The scheme was

valued not in conventional capitalist terms of profit and loss, but in terms of the 'welfare of the nation'.[9] Strasser calculated that additional revenue and savings on benefits generated by the ensuing activity would cover a significant part of the costs, although conservatives (and Social Democrats) condemned it as dangerously inflationary. Hitler, who also feared inflation, saw the scheme scaled down in the autumn, but Strasser had succeeded in associating the NSDAP with energetic anti-unemployment proposals at a critical stage in the electoral struggle. It would appear that the unemployed themselves were only impressed to a limited degree at the polls, but many other Germans were anxious to remove the threatening spectre of mass unemployment.

Hitler's personal contribution to pre-1933 policy-making was at once decisive and diffuse. As seen, he had the final say in matters of detailed policy formulation and his convictions were instrumental in determining the overall tone of policy and of its presentation. However, he did not publish any detailed proposals on a par with the agricultural or 'Work and Bread' programmes, although the pages of *Mein Kampf* give an indication of his longer term objectives, whilst his *Second Book* which was written but not published in 1928 spelled out his thoughts, not least on economic matters, more fully. His views were implicitly Malthusian; limited territory and natural resources placed ultimate constraints on any one people's economic prospects. European economies, he observed, were seeking to overcome these constraints through international trade, but his views on the long-term prospects for trade were similarly pessimistic. As more countries industrialised they would cease to serve as markets for European manufacturers or, in the case of Japan and the USA, would displace European manufacturers in remaining markets. He also feared that individual businesses would put their own commercial interests above collective national interests by opening subsidiary factories in developing countries, thereby reducing the openings for the home economy. War and the conquest of territory were, for Hitler, the Social Darwinistic solution to this perceived problem (see Documents 11, 12, 13).

However, to have become involved in the nuts and bolts of everyday policy would have violated the perception of his own role as leader and unifying point within the movement and, he believed, would have yielded limited dividends. This applied in particular to domestic economic policy where, as he commented, a promise made to one group alienated another. Hitler's own observations on economics focused on the issue of external trade in the manner described above. (Intriguingly, however, during his row with Otto Strasser which ended in the latter's resignation from the NSDAP in 1930, Hitler argued the opposite.) Similarly he was careful to avoid partisanship with regard to social policy. He professed sympathy with workers' grievances under the conditions of liberal capitalism, but also reassured employers at a number of meetings that he would uphold property rights and business interests once in power.

If Hitler published little beyond *Mein Kampf*, he said a great deal. His early speeches targeted the Treaty of Versailles, the SPD and the Jews and as such were standard fare in the nationalist circles of early Weimar Germany. His presentation of the message was, however, unique and effective. As Rainer Zitelmann observes, 'Much of what he said also sounded new and many contemporaries were unsure what to make of this man and his National Socialist Party';[10] or as Zeman remarks, 'What Hitler said mattered far less than how he said it'.[11] He certainly strove to avoid being pinned down as a conventional right- or left-wing politician, observing that: 'The nationalists on the right lacked social awareness, the socialists on the left lacked national awareness' (see also Document 10 and cf with 9).[12] He sought a synthesis of the virtues of both poles while avoiding their vices, but in so doing he adopted vices of a different sort. Racialism was central to his ideological vision and coloured National Socialist policy and behaviour from the outset. His early speeches blamed the Jews for Germany's defeat and associated them with 'international finance capital', but under the influence of Rosenberg and Eckart he soon came to regard Soviet Bolshevism also as a Jewish phenomenon. By 1922, Ian Kershaw remarks, the racial dialectic was central to Hitler's thinking,[13] and as Karl-Dietrich Bracher comments, racist anti-Semitism was 'the one basic principle to which Hitler subscribed deeply, blindly, ruthlessly'.[14]

Not surprisingly, some of the earlier histories of Nazism sought explanations for the overthrow of Weimar in the exposition of these anti-Semitic convictions to a receptive German audience. It is, however, now generally recognised that

Nazi campaigners played down imperialistic and racialist policies during the later Weimar years. Hitler had not altered his views, but understood that to emphasise these particular themes would condemn the NSDAP to a perpetual minority status. Attacks on the republican political system and on class politics (especially Marxism) and programmatic appeals couched in the language of national resurgence were used to far greater effect.

II

If Hitler's contribution to the intellectual history of post-Enlightenment Europe was, to put it kindly, dubious, his record as a propagandist and communicator was outstanding. He developed and refined abilities that were apparent from the beginnings of his political career and wrote perceptively in *Mein Kampf* about the relationship between the orator and his audience and about the impact of mass meetings upon individual attendants (see also Documents 23, 24).[15] On his first appearance at a DAP meeting he impressed the other participants with his rhetorical abilities, which had been first sharpened as a political educator within the post-war army. These skills quickly gave him a crucial edge in the NSDAP's early leadership struggles, for his services were regarded as indispensable, and also subsequently consolidated his authority over the party hierarchy. In Kershaw's words he succeeded in creating 'an inner circle of believers' during his internment at Landsberg and thereafter.[16]

Ultimately, however, Hitler had to appeal to the masses. As he himself put it, the 'first task of propaganda is to win men for the organisation' and 'to win adherents to the idea'.[17] Mass meetings at which Hitler personified the drive to power played the primary role in this process. His ability to empathise with the emotions and expectations of an audience and to hold his listeners' attention for up to two hours (he was no devotee of the 'sound bite') has become almost the stuff of legend and, it is sometimes suggested, legend is the appropriate word. No one seriously casts doubt on Hitler's public speaking abilities, but for all his use of modern transport, including cars and aircraft, to cover an immense amount of ground, most citizens of Weimar never set eyes on the Nazi leader. More often his appeal was indirect, to the point where local Nazi propaganda bills could even misspell his name.

Some of his senior deputies, such as Joseph Goebbels, acquired a reputation as speakers in their own right. As *Gauleiter* of Berlin, Goebbels held a series of meetings distinguished, in Elke Fröhlich's words, 'by boldness, aggression and – extreme effectiveness'.[18] He was a practitioner of provocative publicity, staging events in left-wing strongholds at which violence and intimidation as much as the spoken word ensured that the NSDAP received ample coverage in the city's press. Goebbels also found the courtroom a congenial medium for acquiring publicity. A Member of Parliament from 1928 and therefore immune from imprisonment, he used his newspaper, *Der Angriff*, to vilify political opponents, including Berlin's Deputy Police Chief who happened to be Jewish. True to his watchword – 'no information, just agitation' – he then used ensuing court actions to carry his attacks further in a blaze of press coverage.

Leaders apart, the NSDAP relied on a cadre of speakers to address most meetings. During the 1920s these speakers typically ranged their own districts as enthusiastic amateurs, sowing some of the seed from which the Nazi movement would grow, but with time the Nazis' spoken propaganda became increasingly professional. In Lower Saxony, Jeremy Noakes observes, the *Gau* of South Hanover Brunswick set the launch date for the 1930 election campaign, forwarded a list of potential speakers to national headquarters for ultimate approval, provided these speakers with booklets which detailed propaganda techniques and the NSDAP's main policies, and kept them 'up to date with regular reports on day-to-day events as they happened'.[19] Printed material was controlled with similar care, and poster campaigns – including the sabotage of rival material – were likewise coordinated from the centre, by Goebbels. This particular *Gau* was in no way unique in these respects, and throughout Germany the NSDAP maintained the dynamic of frequent meetings once the election was over; in this it differed markedly from the Weimar parties. Care was taken to ensure that speakers were of an adequate calibre. Local speakers needed appropriate certification to operate on a regional basis, and regional speakers required similar authorisation to perform nationally. Formal examinations ensured that putative speakers were of sufficient quality and that they satisfied the NSDAP's own distinctive brand of political correctness (see Documents 26, 27).

Repeated meetings eventually produced diminishing returns, and the NSDAP consequently strove to entertain and to surround itself with a sense of mystique as much as to cajole or inform. Various forms of military pageantry proved very successful in a highly nationalistic, but largely demilitarised, country. The Nazis did not enjoy a monopoly of quasi-military display, but their SA bands, paramilitary rallies and marches, military gymnastics displays, plays and films outshone the efforts of their rivals (see Document 25). There was also an air of conviction about Nazi militarism which was, perhaps, lacking within republican paramilitary organisations which were, after all, ultimately dedicated to the defence of parliamentarianism. Events such as the Nuremberg Rally, staged annually from 1927, were mounted with particular care. The choreographing of torchlight processions, flag-bearing paramilitaries and the construction of elaborate stage sets provided Hitler and his lieutenants with an imposing demonstration of power, whether imaginary or real. The Nazi flag itself was a remarkable invention. Basically red, with all the obvious connotations thereof, it simultaneously evoked memories of the pre-Weimar Empire through its additional use of white and black. The black was represented by a large swastika within a white circular ground to represent the Aryan racial heritage, although the symbol was and remains a powerful, intimidating symbol in its own right. The Nazi 'Heil Hitler' (literally 'hail to Hitler') greeting was similarly potent to the point where the Communist movement was driven to countering it with the (somewhat problematic) greeting, 'Heil Moskau'. But if the NSDAP's dynamism posed problems for the relatively vigorous left, it eclipsed the efforts of the traditional right and centre. These latter parties were simply not geared psychologically or organisationally to maintaining a constant public profile and what meetings they held were largely restricted to election periods. This laid them open to the twin charges of cynical vote grubbing and overall complacency in a time of grave national emergency, their patriotic protestations to the contrary notwithstanding. As Zeman among others has observed, in much of the centre and right's traditional heartland it was really only the National Socialists who mounted any effective political campaign at all,[20] although the monarchist paramilitary league, the Stahlhelm, could be relatively effective in parts of the northern Protestant countryside (see Document 5).

The storm-troopers of the SA, eventually numbering some 450,000 ill-assorted and often ill-equipped volunteers, were the foot soldiers and the spearhead of day-to-day Nazi propaganda campaigns. As marchers, flag-bearers, election canvassers, carriers of oral propaganda and defenders of the NSDAP's own controversial meetings their contribution was indispensable. However, their prime role was as the purveyors of violence. Staged or spontaneous brawls and various forms of physical intimidation, ranging from individual personal violence to threatening displays of collective strength, had a significant and largely positive impact on the Nazis' public appeal. As Eugen Hadamovsky, later Chief of Broadcasting, commented, 'Propaganda and the graduated use of violence have to be employed together in a skilful manner. They are never absolutely opposed to each other. The use of violence has to be a part of propaganda.'[21] The Nazis, of course, neither invented political violence, nor have they spoken the last word on the matter, but they were skilled exponents of the art. As early as 1922 Hitler foresaw the deployment of the SA to show the left that the NSDAP was 'the future ruler of the street just as it will eventually become the ruler of the state'.[22] This was at once a bold and risky strategy, for the German left had used collective displays of strength to proclaim its dominance of urban strongholds; the SA was in effect to disrupt and even displace this domination wherever possible (see Documents 28–31). In the final years of Weimar the SA's tactics clearly bore fruit as locally recruited, urban SA men succeeded in establishing regular meeting and drinking places, and even soup kitchens and other welfare institutions, in some of the areas which the Communists or Social Democrats had claimed as their own.

However, as intimated earlier, the establishment of a physical presence in left-wing strongholds was only part of the SA's function. The organisation was intended to encapsulate a militant national solidarity to which its militaristic pageantry and (often makeshift) uniforms gave testimony. Zeman regards the SA as, possibly, a more potent propaganda weapon than even

'Hitler's words',[23] and, as Richard Bessel remarks, the dissemination of propaganda by the SA amounted to propaganda in itself.[24]

Joseph Goebbels complained in January 1932 that the NSDAP 'had the best speakers in the world', but lacked a 'nimble and skilful press'.[25] This was no reflection on the quantity of Nazi publications, for in addition to the national flagship paper, the *Völkischer Beobachter*, a national tabloid, the *Illustrierter Beobachter*, and a wide range of regional and local papers were produced. The Strasser brothers controlled their own publishing house, and Nazi organisations, such as the SA and the NSBO, produced their own 'in-house' newspapers during the early 1930s. Most people who were already in the Nazi movement probably read one or other of these publications regularly, but the level of sales to the wider public was disappointing. Sales of the *Völkischer Beobachter*, for instance, were well under 100,000 at the time of the September 1930 electoral breakthrough. The quality of Nazi journalism was, in addition, not outstanding and this seems to have been the target of Goebbels' complaint. Only in terms of layout, the use of banner headlines, photographs and the like did the Nazi papers possess a vigour lacking in many rival papers.

Even so, Hitler regarded ownership of the *Völkischer Beobachter* as important for his party, perhaps for symbolic reasons since all major parties had their own mouthpiece. In addition he was beholden to the conservative press. The latter presented the physical confrontations between the SA and its opponents as a nationalist, defensive struggle by the Nazis' thin brown line against 'red' aggression. Papers controlled by the DNVP's leader, Alfred Hugenberg, were particularly good friends to the Nazis and during joint nationalist/Nazi political campaigns, such as that against the Young Plan, Hitler and his movement were afforded sympathetic coverage. The UFA cinema newsreels, also controlled by Hugenberg, were a further friend, although the relationship soured in the autumn of 1932 after the breakdown of coalition negotiations between Hitler and von Papen. This backing has led historians to ponder on the possible relationship between this form of conservative friendship and Nazi electoral success. Richard Hamilton suggests a positive correlation between the Nazis' urban electoral performance and sympathetic press coverage,[26] and Jürgen Falter provides statistical evidence to confirm that in districts with a right-wing (non-Nazi) press, the

NSDAP tended to do better, all else being equal.[27]

III

There remains the broader question of precisely how far Nazi propaganda did actually contribute to the movement's success. Historians have frequently reflected on the difficulties inherent in establishing an unequivocal causal relationship and in 1980 Bessel suggested that Nazi propaganda was neither particularly distinctive nor outstanding. It simply addressed interests and concerns which potential constituents held before Nazism arrived on the scene.[28] If this sounds slightly tautological, Oded Heilbronner has recently reached comparable conclusions, arguing that in Baden the collapse of Catholic milieus rather than the virtuosity of the NSDAP's propaganda gave the party an entrée into the political life of the region.[29] Clearly, therefore, it would be unwise to overstate the seductive properties of Nazi propaganda, but it would be equally foolish to suggest that the immense efforts that the National Socialists made to sell themselves were irrelevant to their success. As Kershaw remarks, the energy and activism associated with Nazism defined its image even in areas where it was dormant organisationally.[30] Propaganda, it might be said, did as much in its own right to lend substance to National Socialism as it did to transmit the substance of ideology and policy to potential supporters.

The social profile of these potential supporters has always been subject to debate, but a majority view once regarded young, middle-class and female citizens as particularly likely to back the Nazis at the polls and young, middle-class males as most likely to join the movement. That the NSDAP, SA and SS were relatively youthful bodies is clear and Nazi propaganda certainly exalted this youthfulness: 'Make room you old ones!', as Gregor Strasser declared.[31] Hans Mommsen observes that the conventional Weimar parties became, if anything, more committed to conventional ideological positions, thereby widening the rift between generations and providing the NSDAP with valuable space.[32] In elections, however, there is no clear evidence to suggest that young voters in particular backed the NSDAP, and Falter concludes that any such trend was localised and possibly in conflict with the national tendency for older voters to be more strongly predisposed towards the Nazis.[33] Male domination of the Nazi movement remains indisputable, but many classic works suggest that the pageantry and virile militarism of this masculine party turned the heads of German womanhood and delivered up a disproportionate number of female votes for Hitler's movement. The reality was probably otherwise, for, as Falter has demonstrated, women from most backgrounds, in most elections, were slightly less likely to vote Nazi than men.[34] In a recent work Helen Boak has noted that as the SPD's vote declined during the early 1930s it was men rather than women who tended to desert it,[35] to the NSDAP's considerable benefit (see Document 16). All in all, reference to age and gender indicates the breadth and diversity of the NSDAP's appeal, rather than revealing a particular focus on individual target groups.

A strong body of opinion has perceived Nazi propaganda, at least from 1928, as targeted on the middle classes. Bracher, for example, maintained that the NSDAP's mass propaganda 'was directed almost exclusively toward the middle classes', who were thereby mobilised for a 'desperate two-front battle against capital and proletariat'.[36] Zeman concurs, arguing that after a failed attempt to rally the urban population between 1925 and 1928, the Nazis turned their efforts to mobilising the lower middle classes, not least in the countryside. The only other significant propaganda target, Zeman argues, was the unemployed.[37] Peter Fritzsche remarks that the regularity of Nazi meetings in Lower Saxon towns helped to trigger the switch to the NSDAP by the region's middle classes in September 1930.[38] Kershaw has also argued that Nazi ideology and its projection through propaganda was aimed at and appealed to the middle classes. It was 'ideally placed to integrate the heterogeneous middle class on an ideological plane into a movement which could promise to defend sectional interest while claiming to stand above it'.[39] The failure of the 'urban plan' by 1928, he claims, saw the redirecting of propaganda towards the rural and provincial middle classes, with the irrational and mystical side of this propaganda 'a product of the political culture of the German bourgeoisie'.[40]

Despite its popularity such an interpretation has never been universally supported. In his study of Lower Saxony Jeremy Noakes concluded in 1971 that the targets for Nazi propaganda changed on a number of occasions and that, if anything, this propaganda was characterised by its diversity.[41] Early propaganda had not neglected the middle classes, but was aimed 'above all at the workers'.[42] The re-establishment of the NSDAP after the Munich *Putsch* saw priority in Lower Saxony, as elsewhere, accorded to industrial areas, with a commensurate left-wing slant to the propaganda itself.[43] Noakes agrees that in 1928 the NSDAP abandoned this emphasis and paid particular attention to middle-class interests, with rural areas becoming the prime target for propaganda. It was here, he feels, that the Nazis enjoyed their greatest success, but he also observes that they continued to court a wider range of groups, including women and workers. Strasser's 'Work and Bread' speech of May 1932 is seen as especially significant in this regard, for in offering co-operation with the trade unions, among others, he was appealing particularly to SPD voters.[44]

Writing in 1972, Max Kele maintained that the NSDAP's attempts to woo working-class support were of fundamental importance and met with considerable success.[45] His work was greeted with a degree of scepticism for it pre-dated the electoral and membership studies which have since confirmed that the Nazis did, indeed, possess a very large working-class following. There were additional difficulties in his (still controversial) view that salaried staff were essentially part of a broader working class. However, historians have become increasingly predisposed to assert that National Socialist propaganda, after 1928 as much as beforehand, was targeted on as wide a spread of society as possible and not at any particular class or group. Falter contends that the working classes were a key target for Nazi propaganda.[46] In 1989 Jeremy Brown published an intriguing short study into the structure of the Nazi propaganda effort in Berlin. The party's organisation was by no means concentrated in middle-class parts of the city: NSDAP groups in working-class districts or areas held 3,905 meetings between 1928 and 1933, those in middle-class districts held 2,147.[47] Brown argues that the content of Nazi propaganda in the city further confirms that the 'NSDAP wanted to establish its centre of gravity in the working-class districts with a working-class image', although he concludes that this effort ultimately failed.[48] It might therefore appear that middle-class Berlin voted Nazi in spite of the movement's propaganda, but Hamilton's work on the Nazi electorate in the city indicates that this conclusion is a little harsh. The NSDAP received about a quarter of votes cast in working-class parts of the city, and in sum half the votes cast for the NSDAP in Berlin were from these working-class areas.[49] Goebbels, presumably, did not find this disappointing.

On balance, studies of Nazi propaganda which emphasise its middle-class dimension to the virtual exclusion of all else possess several weaknesses. Firstly, to have stressed middle-class interests and to have directed all propaganda in this direction would have violated the basic ideological and programmatic tenets of National Socialism which vigorously opposed class or sectional interest politics; and, as Thomas Childers notes, the Nazis consciously refused to operate as a class party (see also Documents 10, 14, 15).[50] Secondly, it is becoming increasingly apparent that the Nazis, true to their aim of rising above factional politics, directed their propaganda in all its forms at the widest possible range of targets, adjusting its content as and when appropriate. Finally, as will be discussed further in due course, our current understanding of the National Socialists' constituency indicates that it was exceptionally diverse in social terms, suggesting that the NSDAP's propaganda functioned as they would have wished. They intended to mobilise all 'ethnic' Germans, tried to do so and enjoyed a degree of success in crossing class, regional, confessional, gender and age barriers which was unprecedented in German political history.

Notes

1 Barbara Miller Lane and Leila J. Rupp (eds.), *Nazi Ideology before 1933. A Documentation*, Manchester, 1978.

2 *Ibid.*, p. xii.

3 *Ibid.*, p. xv.

4 Quoted in Udo Kissenkoetter, 'Gregor Strasser: Nazi Party Organiser or Nazi Politician?', in Ronald Smelser and Rainer Zitelmann (eds.), *The Nazi Elite*, trans. M. Fischer, Basingstoke, London, 1993, p. 226.

5 Quoted in Lane and Rupp, *Ideology*, pp. 118–19.

6 Quoted in *ibid.*, p. 123.

7 Kissenkoetter, 'Strasser', p. 231.

8 Quoted in Lane and Rupp, *Ideology*, p. 137.

9 Quoted in *ibid.*, p. 144.

10 Rainer Zitelmann, 'Adolf Hitler: The Führer', in Smelser and Zitelmann (eds.), *Nazi Elite*, p. 115.

11 Z. A. B. Zeman, *Nazi Propaganda*, 2nd edn., London, Oxford, New York, 1973, p. 5.

12 Zitelmann, 'Hitler', p. 116.

13 Ian Kershaw, *Hitler*, London, New York, 1991, pp. 23–8.

14 Karl Dietrich Bracher, *The German Dictatorship. The Origins, Structure and Effects of National Socialism*, trans. J. Steinberg, London, 1973, pp. 132–3.

15 Adolf Hitler, *Mein Kampf (My Struggle)*, London, 1938, p. 186 f.

16 Kershaw, *Hitler*, p. 31.

17 Hitler, *Mein Kampf*, p. 233.

18 Elke Fröhlich, 'Joseph Goebbels: The Propagandist', in Smelser and Zitelmann (eds.), *Nazi Elite*, p. 51.

19 Jeremy Noakes, *The Nazi Party in Lower Saxony 1921–1933*, Oxford, 1971, p. 152.

20 Zeman, *Propaganda*, p. 13.

21 Quoted in *ibid.*, p. 13.

22 Quoted in *ibid.*, p. 14.

23 *Ibid.*, p. 18.

24 Richard Bessel, *Political Violence and the Rise of Nazism. The Storm Troopers in Eastern Germany 1925–1934*, New Haven, London, 1984, p. 153.

25 Quoted in Zeman, *Propaganda*, p. 18.

26 Richard Hamilton, *Who Voted for Hitler?*, Princeton, NJ, 1982, pp. 91 f, 123 f, 139 f, 153 f, 162 f, 175 f, 185 f, 190 f, 195 f, 202 f, 206 f, 211 f, 214.

27 Jürgen W. Falter, *Hitlers Wähler*, Munich, 1991, p. 334 ff.

28 Richard Bessel, 'The Rise of the NSDAP and the Myth of Nazi Propaganda', *Wiener Library Bulletin*, 33, 1980, pp. 20–9.

29 Oded Heilbronner, 'The Black Forest: the Disintegration of the Workers' Catholic Milieu and the Rise of the Nazi Party', in Conan Fischer (ed.), *Weimar, the Working Classes and the Rise of National Socialism*, Oxford, 1995, forthcoming.

30 Ian Kershaw, 'Ideology, Propaganda, and the Rise of the Nazi Party', in Peter D. Stachura (ed.), *The Nazi Machtergreifung*, London, Boston, Sydney, 1983, p. 173.

31 Quoted in Bracher, *German Dictatorship*, p. 189.

32 Hans Mommsen, 'National Socialism. Continuity and Change', in Walter Laqueur (ed.), *Fascism: A Reader's Guide. Analyses, Interpretations, Bibliography*, London, 1976, p. 161.

33 Falter, *Wähler*, p. 146 ff.

34 *Ibid.*, p. 136 ff.

35 Helen Boak, 'National Socialism and working-class Women before 1933', in Fischer (ed.), *Weimar*, forthcoming.

36 Bracher, *German Dictatorship*, pp. 203–4.

37 Zeman, *Propaganda*, pp. 26–8.

38 Peter Fritzsche, *Rehearsals for Fascism. Populism and Political Mobilization in Weimar Germany*, New York, Oxford, 1990, p. 207.

39 Kershaw, 'Ideology', p. 175.

40 *Ibid.*, p. 176.

41 Noakes, *Nazi Party*, p. 202.

42 *Ibid.*, p. 18.

43 *Ibid.*, p. 104.

44 *Ibid.*, pp. 213–14.

45 Max H. Kele, *Nazis and Workers. National Socialist Appeals to German Labor 1919–1933*, Chapel Hill, 1972.

46 Falter, *Wähler*, p. 226 f.

47 Jeremy R. S. Brown, 'The Berlin NSDAP in the *Kampfzeit*', *German History*, 7, 1989, pp. 242–4.

48 *Ibid.*, p. 247.

49 Hamilton, *Who Voted?*, p. 91.

50 Thomas Childers, 'The middle classes and National Socialism', in David Blackbourn and Richard J. Evans (eds.), *The German Bourgeoisie. Essays on the social history of the German middle classes from the late eighteenth to the early twentieth century*, London, New York, 1991, p. 320.

4

The organisation of the Nazi movement

In 1919 the infant NSDAP's organisational capacity did not amount to much. Even after Hitler had consolidated his position as leader and attracted sizable audiences to National Socialist meetings in Munich, the NSDAP had not begun to develop the organisational and financial capacity which would be required to take on and overthrow the Weimar Republic. Yet, by the early 1930s, the Nazi movement had been dramatically transformed. Bearing in mind the many decades required by democratic socialist parties to develop sufficient organisational strength to mount a challenge to the existing order and the decidedly gradual and evolutionary development of many other modern popular parties, the rapid emergence of the differentiated and relatively sophisticated organisational apparatus surrounding the NSDAP is remarkable indeed.

Historians have pointed to the role models which Hitler was able to emulate. He was especially impressed by the left-wing mass parties and consciously copied their techniques of organisation as much as he drew on their methods of propaganda and political mobilisation. In this he differed substantially from most of his radical nationalist contemporaries, whose activist and often explicitly right-wing leagues and parties were designed to appeal to particular clienteles, social or ideological, and as often as not behaved in a covert, conspiratorial manner. Hitler had no time for such divisiveness and underhandedness. For him all Germans shared the same objective interests. Only the stupidity and self-interest of the establishment and the capitalist classes had led to

the alienation of the working people from the all-German community; only the devious subversion of the same workers by
Jewish-inspired Marxist agitators had exploited this alienation.
The NSDAP intended to rally the entire ethnic German people
behind itself (see Documents 10, 15).

In the early 1920s, however, this was all far from straightforward. The NSDAP was no stranger to political violence in a
violent country and organised its own paramilitary force in
August 1921: the Gymnastics and Sport Division of the NSDAP.
In November 1921 this was renamed the Storm Division
(*Sturmabteilung* or SA) whose storm-troopers were charged with
protecting National Socialist meetings and even taking the fight
to opponents (see Document 28). Soon enough, however, the
SA's leaders went further and co-operated on their own initiative
with radical right-wing leagues which were plotting the overthrow of the Republic. To make matters even more complicated,
there was covert and not so covert collaboration between these
leagues and the Bavarian army and government. The Bavarians
hoped to use the radical leagues to underpin secession from the
Republic; the leagues hoped to use Bavaria and its rebellious
authorities as a launching pad for the overthrow of the same
Republic, regarding the precedent set by Mussolini in Italy as
most encouraging. Hitler found himself trapped as the gifted
propagandist for this essentially paramilitary and putschist
umbrella organisation; his own party certainly remained a prominent force for political agitation, but was not entirely a free agent.
Ironically it was to take the failure of the November *Putsch* in 1923
to allow Hitler to achieve the supremacy of the party over the
paramilitaries and the beginnings of organisational developments which were to set the NSDAP on the road to 1930.

Even so, the early years of the NSDAP saw Hitler force through
internal organisational reforms which were to be crucial to the
future character of the NSDAP and even to the National Socialist
State. The DAP had operated through a committee chaired by
Anton Drexler within which genuine debate seems to have occurred and within which majority decisions were taken. Hitler's
position became very strong once his oratorical talents were
apparent, but he enjoyed no constitutional right to dictatorial
powers within the party. Indeed, in his own memoirs he claimed
that, while he would not tolerate criticism of his strategy as a

public speaker at this time, he did not interfere in the affairs of other sections of the party. An internal party crisis during mid-1921 was to alter this situation radically and lead to the institution of the Leader Principle (*Führer Prinzip*).

The crisis broke on 11 July when Hitler resigned publicly from the NSDAP in the expectation that his services were indispensable and that he would be able to demand his own price for returning to the fold; and demand it he did. Power was to be centralised, with decisions made in Munich binding on all branches of the party. There was, furthermore, to be no talk of coalition or merger with other radical fringe sects, many of which had sprung up at this time. Such groups were to be encouraged to merge into the NSDAP, thereby losing their own identity whilst allowing the National Socialist movement gradually to obtain a critical mass of members, resources and publicity which each individual fringe group lacked. Most crucially, Hitler demanded complete personal control of the Munich branch so as to allow himself control of the party's ideological development and the final word on organisational and strategic matters. Anton Drexler was aware that he could not match Hitler for commitment, energy and oratorical skills, and in the days following Hitler's resignation the feeling grew within the party at large that Hitler's demands should more or less be met. Hitler's supporters pressed his case to the limit and threatened to create a backlash, but on 29 July a mass meeting of party members voted to accept his ultimatum. Drexler was made Honorary Convener of the party, while Hitler became the effective and absolute leader of an executive committee packed with his own supporters (see Document 35).

The practical organisational consequences of Hitler's triumph were substantial. Any political party witnesses its share of factional infighting and personal rivalry over the years, but Ian Kershaw, among others, has stressed the exceptional degree of instability within the Nazi movement which consisted of 'extremely diverse factions and interests, with strong centrifugal and disintegrative tendencies'.[1] This resulted in particular from the development of numerous personal fiefdoms within the NSDAP whose responsibilities were not always clearly delineated, although this may not have sacrificed efficiency to the degree one might imagine. Hitler made a virtue of the situation, arguing that open struggle allowed the better or stronger individual, institution or idea to triumph (in Social Darwinistic fashion). This form of decision-making, of course, strengthened his role as supreme arbiter; indeed his powers as leader were utterly crucial in staving off organisational disaster. His new-found dominance quickly came to rest on far more than functional indispensability. In December 1920 the NSDAP had acquired a Munich newspaper, the *Völkischer Beobachter* (until August 1919 the *Münchener Beobachter*), which disseminated propaganda and news as the public, semi-official voice of the movement. By the later 1920s daily circulation was extending well beyond its Bavarian base and helped promote a leadership cult which presented Hitler as the embodiment of the National Socialist movement's ideology, programme and wider mission. Certainly he did become a charismatic leader in the sense described by the sociologist Max Weber and while manipulation and propaganda played a role in this, it must be conceded that Hitler himself possessed personal qualities which made his absolute claim to authority credible.

This personification of National Socialism in Hitler, the leader, provided the central point of reference and arbitration for the medley of personalities and auxiliary organisations within the movement at which disputes could be resolved and from which other Nazi leaders derived their own legitimacy and authority. There was no future for any leader within the movement whom Hitler had disowned. Disputes within the National Socialist movement tended, therefore, to be between Hitler's subordinates on the personal level, and any programmatic or ideological revolts within the party or movement against the central authority were generally short-lived. Their instigators either fell back into line, resigned or were expelled. And it had to be so; a successful revolt would have had to challenge Hitler's personal position in the party, which would have placed in question the very essence of National Socialism itself.

However, reference to Hitler alone cannot provide an adequate explanation for Nazism's organisational successes. From his pivotal position he himself understood that a large measure of organisational responsibility had to be devolved to other individuals and to subsidiary bodies and that while the leader would always act as the final arbiter, most day-to-day decisions and activies within the movement would occur far from his gaze. This was not only inevitable, but also acceptable as long as his ultimate personal authority and his claim to represent the embodiment of National Socialism were not challenged.

This principle, as noted earlier, excluded formal co-operation with the other right-wing radical groups which proliferated during the early 1920s. One such was Julius Streicher's German Socialist Party (DSP) which had branches in many parts of Germany, unlike the predominantly Bavarian NSDAP; but in December 1922 the DSP dissolved itself and merged into the NSDAP. The extension of the branch network in this way was a significant coup for the National Socialist Party which increased its membership to 55,000 by November 1923. It also gained some important new leaders, for, in addition to the notorious Streicher whose Nuremberg newspaper, *Der Stürmer*, represented Nazi anti-Semitism at its most scurrilous, the Strasser brothers, Gregor and Otto, entered the NSDAP. Gregor was later to be at the heart of the movement's organisational apparatus as Chief of National Organisation (ROL) in which role he steadily overhauled, adapted and expanded the party bureaucracy during the years of explosive success between 1929 and 1932.

In the immediate term, however, the failure of the Munich *Putsch* in November 1923, the imprisonment of Hitler and the banning and subsequent splintering of the party undermined the movement's organisational coherence. This situation was not unwelcome to Hitler himself for as long as he remained in prison; the emergence of an effective successor would have demonstrated his own dispensability and prejudiced any future reacquisition of control. In the event, Hitler nominated Alfred Rosenberg as interim leader; he was largely ineffectual (as Hitler suspected he would be) and different elements within the Nazi movement pursued distinctive political strategies under a number of different leaders. Those around Gregor Strasser and Erich Ludendorff entered a radical right-wing parliamentary coalition (the German Ethnic Freedom Party or DVFP) as the National Socialist Freedom Party (NSFP), but in the second, December, election of 1924 the latter was able to win just four of the coalition's fourteen seats. Strasser had enjoyed some success in building up the National Socialist movement in northern Germany, whilst Ernst Röhm had established an autonomous paramilitary league in Bavaria, the Frontbann, as a substitute for the banned SA. Following his release from Landsberg in December 1924 and the reaffirmation of his control of the NSDAP (legalised on 4 January 1925 by the Bavarian government and relaunched in Munich on 27 February) Hitler therefore faced various challenges to the concept of the Leader Principle and to his own authority. The 27,000 strong NSDAP was organised in 607 local branches and those far removed from Munich were, as Bracher notes, barely under the control of party headquarters; nor were they usually willing to remit dues.[2]

Hitler responded to the resulting challenges in a variety of ways. Attempts by Röhm to maintain an autonomous role for the reconstituted SA in 1925 were rebuffed, leading to his resignation as SA Commander on 1 May 1925. He was eventually replaced in August 1926 by Franz Pfeffer von Salomon who appeared to accept that the SA was to be subordinate to the party within the National Socialist movement and that it would not cultivate links with other paramilitary organisations. Initially at least, Hitler tolerated a greater degree of pluralism in party affairs. Of the twenty-three party regions only Munich-Upper Bavaria was unreservedly under his control, while Gregor Strasser was allowed considerable organisational autonomy in northern Germany. This situation led to difficulties, however, as Strasser exploited his freedom of action to promote a new Nazi programme developed in co-operation with his brother Otto and the young radical, Joseph Goebbels, which Hitler regarded as inopportune in terms of its timing if not necessarily its contents.

He could not allow this implicit challenge to his authority. Matters came to a head in February 1926 at a meeting of party leaders in Bamberg where he demanded unqualified loyalty from Strasser and the other north German radicals such as Goebbels. The meeting was dominated numerically by south German delegates loyal to Hitler, but in any case the north Germans proved compliant. In return for this both Strasser and Goebbels were given key party offices, the former becoming Chief of the Propaganda Office on 16 September and the latter *Gauleiter* of Berlin in November. Future organisational difficulties were to be resolved through an arbitration committee, the Uschla, whose members were appointed by Hitler. The leader had, therefore, reasserted the unequivocal link between himself and National Socialism. As

Alan Bullock writes of the Bamberg Conference: 'Hitler had played his trump card; without him as leader, there was no movement, and his audience knew it'.[3] Matters were set on a more formal basis during the early summer. In May Munich's supremacy in the movement was established and the primacy of the convener of the Munich group (Hitler) was also laid down as a basic principle. On 30 June the NSDAP's 'Rules of Association' were registered in the Munich District Court, confirming Hitler as leader, independent of the party's executive.

This executive comprised two tiers. The National Directorate consisted of Hitler, Rudolf Hess (Secretary), Franz Xavier Schwarz (Treasurer) and Philipp Bouhler (Secretary General) and functioned as the governing board of the NSDAP. Below it was the Party Directorate, the departmental committees of which handled matters such as propaganda, finance, youth, the party's organisation, the SA and arbitration (the Uschla). Hitler retained a personal link with each committee through the appointment of its convener (*Amtsleiter*) who had delegated powers of leadership as embodied in the Leader Principle; only the Uschla was run on a more collective basis. As each *Amtsleiter* was answerable personally to Hitler the movement was structured functionally on vertical lines with committees possessing their own vertical chain of personal authority. Finance, the party organisation and the associated field of party membership were regarded as key central functions, however, and on 16 September the Party Treasurer, Schwarz, had his considerable powers which he derived from Hitler given greater substance by a legally attested order. During the early 1930s this administrative structure came to function increasingly effectively and simultaneously became still more differentiated. Legal, economic and press sections were among those created.

The figure of Gregor Strasser dominated these changes from 1928. He was confronted with problems born of success. If its membership was just 27,000 in 1925, the NSDAP had come to issue 178,000 party cards by the end of 1929 and 300,000 by the autumn of 1930. This growth continued unchecked well into 1932 and, even allowing for a high rate of turnover, membership remained above half a million in January 1933. Even in late 1929, Peter Stachura estimates that 3,400 party branches were in existence.[4] The NSDAP's days as a fringe grouping were over.

In recognition of this the decision was taken in principle to split the National Administration into two sections. Organisation Department I, under Strasser, would direct the movement's current operations, whilst Department II, under Konstantin Hierl, was charged with formulating longer-term policy for the day when the NSDAP assumed power. Following the electoral triumph of September 1930 this decision was put into effect. One of Strasser's main problems was keeping something of a grip on regional and local party formations which had often been formed spontaneously in towns and villages without any direct involvement from party headquarters. This effort culminated in his reforms of July 1932, which centralised much of the Party Directorate within a framework of Central Divisions and, theoretically, made it accountable to himself within Organisation Department I which now also reabsorbed Department II. This grip on the party made Strasser appear indispensable in matters of policy formation as well as organisation, and Udo Kissenkoetter recently stressed his considerable impact on the party's parliamentary strategy, his control of several internal party newspapers, his substantial influence over the Factory cells (NSBO) as well as over economic and social policy more generally.[5]

However, Martin Broszat has been one of the many historians who has reminded us that Strasser did not really enjoy untrammelled power. Hitler retained ultimate control of the *Gauleiter* (see below) at regional level and at the centre was able to circumvent parts of Strasser's organisational network. In September 1932, for example, he created a National Economic Council which diminished the significance of the economic advisers and their secretariat organised within Strasser's Central Division IV.[6] All in all Hitler reconciled the need for Strasser's guiding hand at the centre with his own desire to act as the final arbiter in party affairs, but only at the price of a certain incoherence and propensity for conflict at the heart of the movement. None the less, the NSDAP became formidable where it really mattered: in its ability to fight election campaigns. Jürgen Falter is among those who have commented on its use of state-of-the-art techniques such as film, air travel and internal party communications which resulted in all party formations 'being able within 24 hours to react to political developments in a unified fashion or, if necessary, with regard to a particular audience'.[7]

Alongside these functionally determined vertical chains of command existed a horizontally ordered pattern of territorial units and it was through these that instructions from headquarters were executed. The Party Region (*Gau*) was the largest such unit, the boundaries of which were coincident with parliamentary constituency boundaries from 1928 onwards. Each was commanded by a *Gauleiter* who had been appointed by Hitler and owed him personal loyalty, although this did not prevent some regional leaders from pursuing their own interests on occasion. The degree of control the centre could exercise over the day-to-day running of the individual *Gaue* was inevitably limited. During 1931 and 1932 the Party District (*Kreis*), which accorded with state districts, was created, below which was the Party Branch and then a grassroots network of tenement cells (*Hauszellen*), street cells (*Strassenzellen*) and strong points (*Stützpünkte*).

II

The party and its hierarchy constituted the political and organisational core of the Nazi movement. However, the movement also possessed a range of ancillary institutions whose members were not necessarily in the party itself. These carried out specialised functions or addressed the particular needs of a certain social group, but in addition to this the National Socialists became heavily committed within organisations which were not Nazi as such, white-collar trade unions and student unions being cases in point. The breadth of organisations and interests thereby covered brought considerable numbers of Germans into contact with Nazism who might not have joined the party itself, at least in the first instance, and formed a genuine social as well as parliamentary political movement.

Of institutions directly subordinate to Hitler and the party, the SA was the most significant numerically and functionally. During the Third Reich it was to be eclipsed by the SS, but apart from functioning as a personal bodyguard for Hitler and senior Nazi leaders, the SS had no particularly distinctive role during Weimar. It was limited in size and, despite its image as an elitist body which could and did poach members from the SA, it was subordinated to the SA within the National Socialist command structure. The SA's membership grew from around 30,000 in August 1929, to 60,000 in November 1930, 100,000 in January 1931, 290,941 in January 1932 and then to a peak of 445,279 members in August, after which it declined slightly to 425,000 in January 1933 just before Hitler took office as Chancellor. It possessed its own hierarchical command structure which closely resembled that of the army and from 1931 the territorially organised corps (*Gruppen*) created new subordinate units as recruitment and expansion demanded. The greater part of the SA's rank-and-file membership did not belong to the party – for this majority the SA was National Socialism, albeit with Hitler always recognised as leader – but the physical protection, day-to-day political campaigning, the propaganda displays and the terrorising or intimidation of political rivals which the SA carried out were invaluable to the movement as a whole. That said, friction between the SA and the party's leadership created a fault line within the movement's organisation which ran from the centre in Munich right down to the most local level. Hitler's insistence that the SA be subordinate to the party leadership and particularly to himself had brought about Röhm's resignation as SA commander in 1925, but had not ultimately resolved this quarrel. Many SA leaders remained convinced that their paramilitarism and not party politics represented the essence of National Socialism and this triggered constant demarcation disputes between themselves and party officials over finance, discipline and the organisation of events, or on personal grounds.

These disputes became particularly intense during the autumn of 1930, notably in Berlin, as SA commanders were refused places on the NSDAP's list of parliamentary candidates. The SA's Regional Commander for Eastern Germany, Walther Stennes, became the focus of this dissent. He resented the party's domination of Nazi finances which, he argued, was starving both the SA as an institution and its individual, impoverished members of desperately needed resources. Perhaps more crucially, with the impatience typical of a paramilitary adventurer, he claimed that the NSDAP's failure to win the September 1930 elections outright demonstrated the futility of Hitler's parliamentary road to power. Hitler succeeded in quelling this dissent for a time by travelling personally to Berlin and talking with SA leaders and men, but ironically it was the return of Röhm as Chief of Staff of the SA in January 1931 which ultimately resolved these difficulties. In the short term there was an outright revolt by Stennes and his followers in Berlin and parts of north-eastern Germany, not least against Röhm and his personal entourage; their reputation for corruptness, homosexuality and criminal violence offended some established SA commanders who presumably advocated treason of a more respectable kind. In any event the revolt rapidly fizzled out and Röhm, despite his own preference for action, steered the SA clear of any putschist adventures. Loyalty to Hitler and recognition of the scale of the NSDAP's electoral triumphs persuaded him to stay his hand, at least until Hitler was in power. Thereafter the old disputes flared up again. Röhm was to demand the pre-eminence of the SA in military matters (a longstanding SA ambition) and the predominance of the military over the civilian politicians – demands which were to contribute to his own death at the hands of the SS in mid-1934.

Of the other specialist National Socialist institutions those operating in the agricultural economy and in the workplace have been identified as the most important. Richard Walther Darré presided over an Agricultural Affairs Bureau within party headquarters during the early 1930s. It assumed a specialist role within regional and local party formations, providing expert commentary on agricultural affairs, speakers for rural areas and extensive coverage of agrarian matters through Darré's own paper, the *National-Sozialistische Landpost*, various local journals and sections in regional party newspapers. How far this effort created, and how far it accompanied an upsurge of support for National Socialism in Protestant rural Germany remains an open question, but during 1931 and 1932 agricultural politics and National Socialist politics in Protestant rural Germany became thoroughly enmeshed, if not quite identical. As well as setting up their own specialist organisations, the Nazis penetrated and often came to dominate non-Nazi interest groups. One such was the Reich, or National, Land League which became closely involved with the Nazi movement through the entry of National Socialists into its ranks. This form of infiltration was not confined only to agricultural groups. The medical profession, for example, became heavily influenced by the Nazi movement. Michael Kater estimated that doctors were over-represented in the Nazi Party by a factor of three by the end of Weimar and that 45 per cent joined during the Third Reich.[8] The willingness of established members of the professions to lend support to the National Socialists in this way oiled its organisational effort considerably in as far as the NSDAP was often able to exploit pre-existing professional and occupational associations rather than necessarily having to create its own institutions from scratch.

The creation of an organised presence in the factories was less spectacularly successful and has been more or less ignored by many writers. Martin Broszat has been among those historians of National Socialism who have stressed the importance of the National Socialist Factory Cell Organisation (NSBO) for the movement during the early 1930s.[9] It was, admittedly, something of a Cinderella which received little in the way of finance or encouragement from headquarters until 1931. Individual factory cells were set up at the grass roots by groups of north German workers and salaried staff, while an organisational focus was provided in Berlin at least by a 'Secretariat for Workers' Affairs' run by Reinhold Muchow within Goebbels' *Gau* Directorate. Only in the spring of 1931 did Gregor Strasser establish the National Socialist Factory Cell Division (RBA) at headquarters in Munich and only in September were factory politics given prominence in national Nazi propaganda with the launching of the 'Into the Factories Campaign' or HIB-Aktion. Thereafter, however, the NSBO came in Gunther Mai's estimation to resemble an authentic trade union in many respects and by late 1932 it contained more than 250,000 members (see Document 55).[10] It assumed social functions, participated in strikes over economic grievances and became a minority force in workers' politics which neither the powerful socialist-inclined Free Trade Unions nor the much weaker communist oppositional unions could ignore. In practice its behaviour resembled that of the socialist unions more closely than that of the communist, and in 1933 the Free Unions opened tentative negotiations with it over possible co-operation in a National Socialist governed Germany. As it happened the Nazi authorities liquidated the Free Trade Unions in May 1933 after a campaign of terror waged against them by the SA, and it rapidly became clear that there was no room even for a Nazi employee-based union such as the NSBO in the Third Reich. The corporatist German Labour Front (DAF) which purportedly accommodated the interests of employer and employee, manager and managed, within each sector of the economy and within individual firms and plants, was to prevail. None the less, during the closing years of the Republic the National Socialist movement had possessed an organised presence within the labour movement, the ethnic (*völkisch*) socialism of which evidently appealed to some workers during those troubled times.

It is clear that the complexity of the National Socialist movement and the highly personalised nature of authority within it provided ample scope for rivalry and conflict. The SA and the Party Organisation clashed over fundamental issues of policy. The German Women's Order (DFO), which was affiliated to the party, clashed with the NSDAP's own Women's Group, the NSF, during the early 1930s as each struggled to become organisationally dominant in this particular area. The personal ambitions and indeed the personality of the DFO's leader, Elsbeth Zander contributed to the tension, and more generally personal conflict was prone to flare up between individuals within particular organisations. Even so, it remains indisputable that the National Socialist movement succeeded in creating an organisational apparatus capable of collecting and deploying considerable financial resources, of outpointing its rivals in the dissemination of written, verbal and visual propaganda, of attracting a mass membership, of creating or infiltrating special interest associations and, of course, capable of attracting the largest, most broadly-based electoral following seen to that date in German history. If the SPD had succeeded in creating a 'State within the State' during the imperial era, then, partly in conscious emulation of the Social Democrats, the National Socialists had achieved the same by the end of the Weimar period.

III

All of this is well understood and has received extensive treatment in the existing literature, but explanations for this spectacular achievement vary. It is recognised that some of Hitler's lieutenants possessed particular talents as organisers, propagandists and the like, and it is further recognised that these leaders generally stuck at their specific tasks. None, even if or when they fell out with Hitler, believed they had the overall capacities necessary to lead the movement and thus to replace him. However, while the existence of a capable senior leadership was undoubtedly a prerequisite for the growth and success of the National Socialist movement, it does not provide an adequate explanation.

Two further factors suggest themselves: the quality of the NSDAP's local leadership and the degree of enthusiasm and commitment found throughout the Nazi movement during the later Weimar years. With regard to the quality of its local cadres the NSDAP was very much a beneficiary of the age in which it grew up. Over a period of decades the SPD and the trade union movement had evolved competent systems of management which eventually became self-sustaining and even an end in themselves. Organised socialism evolved partly through trial and error, but also, it has been suggested, in part through the training and experience provided to willing and unwilling male Germans within the imperial army. Thereafter, working within the existing order and gaining further know-how thereby, the Social Democratic movement had time and (it hoped) history on its side. Whatever Hitler's views on history he was not a patient man and the failed *Putsch* of November 1923 had provided a sufficient lesson in the risks of trial and error. Germany's wartime experience and post-war military situation, however, provided the National Socialists with a potential solution to this dilemma. The carnage of war had necessitated numerous promotions to junior officer and non-commissioned rank, and with the coming of peace and demobilisation there were many tens of thousands of younger male Germans from a wide variety of middle-, lower middle- and even working-class backgrounds who had acquired the capacity to handle large numbers of subordinates in circumstances where failure or incompetence could result in death or disaster. It might be added that the war had also produced a generation of younger males who had served as private soldiers and were conditioned to obey orders from their superiors, although it was as much their children as they themselves who joined the Nazi movement. Francis Carsten, and more recently Richard Hamilton, have argued that the embittered antirepublicanism of these demobilised junior leaders led many into the *Freikorps* and subsequently to the National Socialists.[11] Former staff officers, field officers and NCOs offered the Nazis a potential organisational cadre of exceptional quality and experience with which to run a militarised political movement in the far less exacting circumstances of peacetime.

This brings us on to the question of commitment and motivation. Bullock notes that even before the September 1930 electoral breakthrough the core of the movement was 'prepared to meet greater demands on their time and pockets than any other German party'.[12] Hans Mommsen estimates that this core of activists numbered some 300,000 in 1932 in a party considerably larger,[13] but despite the corollary of a high level of membership turnover there can be no serious doubt that this dedication was indeed present in good measure. Similarly Jeremy Noakes and William Sheridan Allen have observed that, during Nazism's formative years in Lower Saxony, there were prominent individuals who played outstanding and self-sacrificing roles which contributed decisively to the development of the party.[14]

Turning to finance, small donations often paid in kind or volunteer services provided free of charge, admission charges to meetings, the membership dues (which rose from a few pfennig in the 1920s to 1RM per month by the early 1930s), special levies for particular projects, the compulsory insurance scheme to care for and compensate injured SA members (of 20pf per month paid by all party members from autumn 1930), and the systematic collection of donations from sympathisers all added up to answer the question, 'Who paid Hitler?' To this one might add the derelict buildings put at the movement's disposal on condition they renovated them – which they did using the labour and skills of unemployed storm-troopers – the revenue from National Socialist economic enterprises, such as the Sturm cigarette factory, and even the seasonal agricultural work sometimes given to destitute SA and party members on a preferential basis which helped keep them loyal to, working for and even contributing to the movement. Support from wealthy corporations or individuals, such as funding for the SA from I. G. Farben, was a drop in the bucket when set against the movement's needs and expenditure (see Documents 36, 37, 41).

This view of Nazi finances is widely accepted today, but the principles underlying this somewhat *ad hoc*, grass-roots funding of a mass movement deserve closer examination. Republican contemporaries were, understandably, scathing critics of

National Socialist ideology, but they were mistaken to write off the Nazi movement as being driven solely or even primarily by crassly wrongheaded utopianism or millenarianism. The Republic's welfare system, upgraded as recently as 1927, was in complete disarray from mid-1930 onwards. A contributory system, it was hit by falling receipts and simultaneously rising expenditure once unemployment in Germany began to surge. The independent sector of small businessmen and peasant farmers were also exposed increasingly to bankruptcy and ruin as Germany slid into depression from 1929; indeed falling world price levels had put the German farming economy in trouble well before the general slump began. Forced auctions and dispossessions had become commonplace in rural Germany. Whether the scale of the economic catastrophe was of the German government's making or the result of international forces, the upshot was widespread destitution, misery, outrage and fear (see Documents 49, 50). For the National Socialists the crisis was at once an immense political opportunity and, it seems, the spur to a considerable and genuine collective effort to ameliorate the disaster. The National Socialist women's groups, the SA and party formations mounted a relatively well-coordinated effort to collect and redistribute food, second-hand clothing and even cash which supplied Nazi-run soup kitchens, helped finance emergency hostel accommodation and made possible the holding of Christmas parties and similar festive events. For many, therefore, National Socialism came to represent a means of tackling the crisis in a concrete way and, of course, a means of being seen by the wider community while out and about doing good works (see Documents 38–44). The Nazis' shadow (welfare) state could assume comic dimensions, not least when party branches and officials, women's groups and SA units quarrelled over the distribution of resources and over recognition for their particular efforts in this field, but it was none the less an invaluable propagandistic tool which did also achieve concrete results. Bodies such as the National Socialist People's Welfare (NSV), founded in Berlin in September 1931, provided an organisational focus for this welfare effort well before it acquired an official role in welfare, and ultimately racial, policy in the Third Reich. The Communist movement for one grudgingly admitted this and also observed that the idealistic streak in National

Socialism contributed to its drive and determination, thereby enhancing the movement's organisational coherence.

It would, of course, be a grave error to regard this enthusiasm and idealism as innocent in character. The National Socialists were both a product and an instigator of the gathering darkness of late Weimar Germany. The Nazis' behaviour was not dissimilar to that of the apocryphal (and not always so apocryphal) firereaiser who, as a member of the local volunteer fire brigade, fights the very fires he has started. The National Socialists never made any secret of their desire to dismantle parliamentary democracy and to abolish a wide range of the legal and civil rights which had been granted by or wrested from government in Germany over the centuries. The SA and other elements of the movement flouted the law and undermined the orderly working of society in a multitude of ways; and, not least, they contributed to the atmosphere of tension, fear and hatred which pervaded Weimar's dying years. While the National Socialists' anti-Semitism did not rank decisively in their late-Weimar propaganda it was hardly a secret either. The Germans who kept the National Socialist movement functioning on the ground, whether in the dispensing of material aid or in the local collecting of dues, holding of meetings or everyday electoral work, were at best indifferent to the threat posed by National Socialism to individual liberty; many actively welcomed the demise of republican democracy for reasons rooted in the Weimar experience or in earlier times. Virtues as diverse as compassion, idealistic millenarian optimism, organisational prowess and diligence in work coalesced with fear, hatred, anguish and long-held prejudices to create the drive and mass enthusiasm which underpinned the National Socialists' organisational effort.

Whether this dynamic movement could have sustained itself in the longer term is another matter. Historians, such as Hans Mommsen, have noted the frictions, inconsistencies and bureaucratic deficiencies which threatened to undermine its existence.[15] It could be argued that the idealism and commitment of many individual Nazis compensated for these shortcomings, but this idealism too probably only had a limited shelf-life. Hitler never contemplated a long-term role for National Socialism within the Weimar Republic. The energy and effort found within the movement was directed towards the fastest possible destruction of the Republic through victory at the ballot box by any means available, and with the failure to gain decisive electoral successes during the spring and summer of 1932, the commitment of individual members began to fade somewhat. By January 1933 the National Socialist movement was fraying visibly at the edges as financial difficulties, insubordination and the resignation of leading figures contributed to the oncoming collapse. The most notable resignation was that of the Chief of National Organisation, Gregor Strasser, in December 1932 after he had dared to suggest that the Nazis might have to accept a role within a modified Weimar system rather than take over bag and baggage. Hitler's appointment as Chancellor on 30 January prevented this crisis overwhelming the movement and reducing it to organisational and political turmoil.

Notes

1 Ian Kershaw, *Hitler*, London, New York, 1991, p. 39.

2 Karl Dietrich Bracher, *The German Dictatorship. The Origins, Structure and Effects of National Socialism*, trans. J. Steinberg, London, 1973, p. 173.

3 Alan Bullock, *Hitler and Stalin. Parallel Lives*, London, 1991, p. 170.

4 Peter D. Stachura, *Gregor Strasser and the Rise of Nazism*, London, Boston, Sydney, 1983, p. 72.

5 Udo Kissenkoetter, 'Gregor Strasser: Nazi Party Organiser or Weimar Politician?', in Ronald Smelser and Rainer Zitelmann (eds.), *The Nazi Elite*, trans. M. Fischer, Basingstoke, London, 1993, pp. 229–30.

6 Martin Broszat, *The Hitler State. The foundations and development of the internal structure of the Third Reich*, trans. J. W. Hiden, London, New York, 1981, pp. 52–4.

7 Jürgen W. Falter, 'War die NSDAP die erste deutsche Volkspartei?', in Michael Prinz and Rainer Zitelmann (eds.), *Nationalsozialismus und Modernisierung*, Darmstadt, 1991, p. 46.

8 Michael Kater, *The Nazi Party. A Social Profile of Members and Leaders, 1919–1945*, Oxford, 1983, pp. 112–13.

9 Broszat, *Hitler State*, pp. 40–2, 47–8.

10 Gunther Mai, 'National Socialist Factory Cell Organisation and German Labour Front . . .', in Conan Fischer (ed.), *Weimar, the Working Classes and the Rise of National Socialism*, Oxford, 1995, forthcoming.

11 Francis Carsten, *The Rise of Fascism*, London, 1967, p. 232. Richard Hamilton, *Who Voted for Hitler?*, Princeton, 1982, pp. 445–47.

12 Bullock, *Hitler and Stalin*, p. 184.

13 Hans Mommsen, *Die verspielte Freiheit. Der Weg der Republik in den Untergang 1918 bis 1933*, Frankfurt-am-Main, Berlin, 1990, p. 355.

14 Jeremy Noakes, *The Nazi Party in Lower Saxony 1921–1933*, Oxford, 1971, pp. 122–4. William Sheridan Allen, *The Nazi Seizure of Power. The Experience of a Single German Town 1930-1935*, London, 1966, pp. 25–6.

15 Mommsen, *Freiheit*, pp. 359–60.

5

The formation of the Nazi constituency: the middle classes

I

It has never been seriously doubted that middle-class Germans made up a very significant proportion of the Nazi constituency and that their support resulted from a fundamental antipathy to parliamentary republicanism, or from their experiences during the republican era. These middle classes were deprived of familiar political landmarks following defeat and the collapse of the monarchy in November 1918. Comprising just over half the country's population, they included people with very divergent customs, lifestyles and politics, and their response to the Empire's demise was similarly diverse. Some middle-class politicians and voters welcomed the advent of parliamentary government and participated actively in the creation of Weimar. However, even most of these citizens had expected change to come via support for a victorious war effort and in the form of a constitutional monarchy; instead democracy was the child of defeat and national humiliation. Furthermore, it would be fair to say that most middle-class Germans were unenthusiastic about parliamentarianism on any terms and regarded the new Republic with reserve or open hostility. Some, exhausted by the war and often exasperated by the imperial government's maladroit handling of it, took an initially passive, even fatalistic, attitude. Others were appalled at the suddenness of defeat and revolution and were genuinely apprehensive as to what Social Democratic government might betoken. Developments in the emerging Soviet Union seemed to provide disturbing parallels with their own country's circumstances.

Events were soon to prejudice middle-class attitudes still further. The Social Democratic administration saw its immediate tasks as establishing parliamentary government on a constitutional basis, dealing with the logistical and practical consequences of defeat and reaching a tolerable peace settlement with the victor powers. However, this seemingly pragmatic approach triggered a series of violent responses as well as containing within itself the seeds of future disaster. The violence came from the radical left and right as they clashed intermittently with one another, turned on the government or defended it as time and circumstances dictated. These violent birth agonies persisted until the end of 1923 and left an indelible stain on the character of the Republic which was neither forgiven nor forgotten by the participants in the turmoil or by the victims of it (see Documents 17, 25).

Many middle-class Germans took the view that the troubles were a consequence of Social Democratic and republican government and not, as was the case, a product of opposition to Weimar. It was particularly ironic that in its frantic attempts to stabilise the military, economic and administrative situation the Social Democratic government turned for help and expertise to the institutions of imperial Germany, thereby according them a powerful role in the new Republic. Their survival did much to shape middle-class perspectives and made some sort of counter-revolution, if not a literal return to the days of Empire, a practical possibility. These domestic problems combined with the perceived humiliation of Germany by the victor powers at Versailles, which was compounded by allied military occupation of the Rhineland and especially the French occupation of the Ruhr District in January 1923. Most Germans attributed the hyper-inflation of that year to the peace provisions – not least reparations and the Ruhr affair – and, largely forgetting the contribution of the imperial wartime government to the string of disasters, heaped blame on the republican politicians who had signed the peace treaty.

Middle-class politics began to shift rightwards and individual voters turned increasingly to parties which were indifferent or hostile towards the Republic. The class composition of most major Weimar parties was too heterogeneous to allow any particularly meaningful discussion of changing middle-class preferences at this point, but certain developments merit attention. In January 1919 elections to the National Assembly saw the pro-republican parties take 72.4 per cent of the votes cast, of which the largely middle-class German Democratic Party (DDP) polled 18.6 per cent. But as soon as June 1920, after the signing of the peace treaty, the republicans polled just 43.6 per cent in the first parliamentary elections, within which total the DDP scored only 8.3 per cent. Clearly middle-class voters were abandoning this unequivocal supporter of parliamentary government in droves and they were never to return in significant numbers.

The two parliamentary elections of 1924 confirmed the minority status of the republican parties as well as a general shift to the right. The DNVP, as the main anti-republican conservative party, saw its vote double from 10.3 per cent in 1919 to 20.5 per cent in December 1924, and a *völkisch* coalition which included the NSDAP was also able to make a minor impact at the polls. At the same time the Marxist vote, which became fundamentally divided between the republican SPD and the anti-parliamentary KPD, fell noticeably – from 45.5 per cent in 1919 to just 35.3 per cent by December 1924. It recovered temporarily to 40.5 per cent in 1928, but was typically around 37 per cent thereafter. The presidential elections of 1925, which followed the death of the Social Democratic President Ebert, confirmed the tenuousness of republican sentiment. On the second ballot the wartime leader Field Marshal Paul von Hindenburg who, along with Ludendorff, had presided over Germany's road to disaster from 1916, was voted President of the Republic. Many voters evidently preferred a monarchist President, among them broad swathes of the middle-class Protestant electorate.

The national elections of May 1928 delivered a mixed message to the supporters of the Republic. The mainstay of republican politics, the SPD, did well, polling almost 30 per cent as against 26 per cent in December 1924. The Social Democrats consequently re-entered government for the first time since autumn 1923, and the Social Democrat Hermann Müller headed a cabinet which included the Catholic and liberal parties. The SPD's acceptance once again of governmental authority came as a relief to republicans, socialist and non-socialist, and this time the political and economic climate appeared altogether more propitious than during the Social Democrats' earlier periods in office.

Reparations and the wider conditions of the Versailles Treaty still posed problems, but through the efforts of her long-serving Liberal Foreign Minister, Gustav Stresemann, Germany had been accepted as a member of the international community and had obtained diplomatic, military and financial concessions from the victor powers. A ready supply of foreign capital, largely from the USA, had contributed to an economic recovery which saw output and living standards reach 1913 levels, and in political life the open insurrection and terror of the early 1920s appeared now to be a thing of the past.

The radical anti-republicans of the far left and right had made no great impact in the elections, but there were none the less some worrying signs of a more subtle sort. It was seen in Chapter 1 that President von Hindenburg and much of the establishment were less than overjoyed to have the SPD back in office and in response sought to enhance the constitutional role of the President at the expense of Parliament and the electorate. However, even in 1928 the electorate itself displayed limited enthusiasm for the Republic. A quarter did not vote at all, producing the lowest turnout in any Weimar election, while fewer than half the remainder voted for pro-republican parties. To the left the Communists gained slightly, but to the centre and right an altogether more insidious and ultimately destructive process was underway. Support for the Catholic parties, the republican DDP, the right-liberal DVP and the conservative DNVP fell both relatively and absolutely with many of these lost votes benefiting various middle-class special interest parties.

These small parties represented a diversity of regional and socio-economic interests, some defending the relatively wealthy, others the victims of past economic turmoil and others the first victims of the approaching economic storm, the farming population. In supporting such parties many middle-class voters were maintaining a pattern of behaviour which had originated in the imperial era and never really died out in Weimar. The imperial constitution had limited the Reichstag's powers and bolstered those of the Emperor, his Chancellor and his cabinet to the point where lobbying on behalf of sectional interests developed as one of the more immediately plausible forms of party political behaviour. Efforts to create a broadly based middle-class party in Weimar failed, and as Frank Domurad observed, middle-class support for the centre-right Weimar parties was granted 'in an almost contractual fashion'.[1] In similar vein Jeremy Noakes remarked that the inability of the DNVP to prevent or solve the mounting agricultural crisis in 1928 precipitated desertions by its voters to narrow interest parties and also encouraged support for anti-parliamentary, activist groupings such as the Landvolk.[2] Larry Eugene Jones's conclusion that 'it becomes immediately apparent that the German middle parties were experiencing severe integrational difficulties well before the outbreak of the world economic crisis or the rise of National Socialism'[3] therefore seems highly apposite and the conservative DNVP suffered similar problems. All in all, Thomas Childers observes, about a third of middle-class voters had already abandoned their traditional conservative and liberal parties before the onset of the Great Depression.[4]

In the face of this worrying trend, the established parties of the right and centre began to reassess their ethos and wider political role. There was a general movement rightwards, accelerated by the election of Alfred Hugenberg as leader of the DNVP in October 1928, the appointment of Ludwig Kaas as Centre Party leader in December and the death of the DVP's Gustav Stresemann in October 1929. More significant, perhaps, was a widespread desire within these parties to make good the fractiousness which had hitherto plagued Weimar politics, leading *inter alia* to the amalgamation of the DDP and the *Jungdeutsche Orden* in 1930 as the German State Party (DStP), but this attempt, like all others, failed to impress the German electorate.

The collapse of Müller's cabinet in March 1930, after its failure to agree on a strategy for tackling the soaring deficit in the social security budget, and the failure of his successor, Brüning, to assemble a parliamentary coalition capable of pursuing tough financial policies (yet excluding Hugenberg's DNVP on the right and the SPD on the left) led to early elections in September 1930. These elections were fought in a poisonous political and social atmosphere which boded ill for the more moderate republican parties as voters were given the chance to comment on the deepening economic crisis. Labour relations had deteriorated during 1928 and 1929, particularly in the Ruhr metal industry, but an attempt in 1929 by Duesterberg of the Stahlhelm and Hugenberg of the DNVP to use the reparations question as a pretext for an attack on the Weimar constitution was of greater significance. The precise issue focused on the Young Plan which moderated reparations terms and to which the German government agreed; the right, however, regarded the payment of reparations on any basis as treason. The resulting referendum ended in a humiliating defeat for the DNVP-led National Solidarity Movement, but the involvement of the NSDAP in the campaign gave this small party exposure and respectability on an unprecedented scale. Furthermore, by relating Germany's burgeoning economic and social crisis to the terms of the peace settlement and subsequent foreign policy, the campaign in effect broadcast the NSDAP's central message to a wide and increasingly receptive audience. State and local elections during 1929 and 1930 saw some significant Nazi advances.

II

As the votes were counted, it became clear that the NSDAP had scored an electoral triumph on 14 September 1930; its share of the poll soared from the 2.6 per cent of 1928 to 18.3 per cent. Much contemporary opinion, and many distinguished writers subsequently, argued that the rallying of the Protestant middle-class vote under a single banner had begun, for the DVP's and DNVP's share of the vote had halved, from 8.7 to 4.7 per cent and 14.2 to 7.0 per cent respectively. A rise in (middle-class) electoral participation seemed to explain the rest of the NSDAP's success. The July 1932 election appeared to confirm this hypothesis, for the remaining Protestant liberal vote disintegrated and support for the middle-class splinter parties (discussed earlier) tumbled from a 1930 tally of 13.8 per cent to just 2 per cent as the NSDAP's vote surged to 37.4 per cent. The Nazi party's membership records contained in the *Partei-Statistik* told a similar tale, suggesting that a clear majority of paid-up supporters were middle-class. In 1969, therefore, Karl-Dietrich Bracher's conclusion in *The German Dictatorship* that the NSDAP's 'essential base' was 'among the petty-bourgeois, middle-class and small landholding groups which had been hardest hit by the outcome of the war, the economic crisis, and the structural changes of modern society',[5] attracted no serious criticism in the light of the available electoral and membership evidence. When, in 1989, Hans Mommsen published *Die verspielte Freiheit* (*Freedom Squandered*), he acknow-ledged that National Socialism's constituency was more broadly based than had been previously believed, but observed that the switch of voters from the bourgeois parties to the NSDAP 'showed that a large proportion above all of the bourgeois *Mittelstand* (middle classes) was not prepared to come to terms and not capable of coming to terms with the political circum-stances of post-war Germany' (see Documents 45–47).[6]

With the strength of (Protestant) middle-class support for the Nazi movement not in doubt, historians and social scientists have developed a range of explanations for why so fateful a shift in political preferences might have occurred. At the very outset the emergence of National Socialism, like fascism more generally, demanded theoretical lines of analysis which transcended the impact of day-to-day politics. Such analysis has usually posited close links between Nazism's character and its middle-class con-stituency, examining both middle-class motivation for turning to the NSDAP and the role of National Socialism itself as some form or other of bourgeois *rassemblement*.

Marxist-Leninists accepted at root Lenin's dictum that in the politics of the class struggle, 'There is nothing between dictator-ship of the bourgeoisie and dictatorship of the proletariat; the dream of another, third way is the reactionary lament of the petty bourgeoisie'.[7] However, there was none the less an awareness that the sociology of fascist parties' constituencies made them more than merely another tool of the big bourgeoisie. The Ger-man Communist, Clara Zetkin, argued in June 1923 that because of the character of its mass support fascism contained elements 'which could become extremely uncomfortable, yes, even dangerous, for bourgeois society'[8] (bourgeois here referring to the capitalist elites); while her contemporary, the Comintern official Karl Radek claimed that 'fascism was indeed the socialism of the petit bourgeoisie'.[9] In the final analysis, however, Marxist-Leninists have never renounced their instrumentalist view of fascism. Its middle-class following served as a pawn in the capi-talist game plan, even if the pawn tried occasionally to run amok.

Others have argued that fascism's constituency provides the key to its definition. In 1923 the Italian theorist Luigi Salvatorelli asserted that fascism constituted 'an independent movement of the disgruntled middle and lower-middle classes' rather than an instrument of capitalism.[10] After the Second World War, in the United States, first Talcott Parsons and then Seymour Martin Lipset published works which also perceived Nazism, like fascism, as an autonomous lower middle-class movement which represented the interests of pre-industrial elements in particular.[11] Rather than arising out of a crisis of capitalism, Nazism was the product of a crisis within the pre-capitalist elements of society fomented by the development of capitalism itself. As Lipset observed in *Political Man*, 'The typical Nazi voter in 1932 was a middle-class self-employed Protestant who lived either on a farm or in a small community, and who had previously voted for a centrist or regionalist political party strongly opposed to the power and influence of big business and big labor.'[12]

Lipset's *Political Man* was first published in 1959, since when a consensus has developed around the view that National Socialism assembled its (middle-class) constituency within the context of a broader crisis within German capitalist society itself. The theories advanced have been diverse, occasionally contradictory but more often complementary, and can only be considered relatively briefly here. In 1967 Francis Carsten doubted the validity of explanations for fascism which refer to particular class interests alone, arguing instead that it was a reaction to a wider crisis: 'There is more truth in the assertion that this rise was due to a malaise, a maladjustment of capitalist society, the victims of which were the lower middle classes more than any other social group'.[13] The structure of Weimar's middle class lends credence to this hypothesis. Even between the wars many observers took with a pinch of salt the claim that the lower middle classes were being squeezed out of existence. Ludwig Preller and Theodor Geiger remarked on the rise of the new middle class of technicians, white-collar staff and public employees, which compensated for the structural decline of parts of the old middle classes. In addition, parts of the skilled working class were reportedly faring increasingly well; so much so that Geiger suggested that some workers were securing jobs or acquiring lifestyles which were essentially middle-class.[14]

However, in addition to the political traumas of the middle classes, salaried staff suffered periodic cuts in income during the Weimar era and even a degree of unemployment during the Depression, while public servants reacted with great bitterness to cuts in salary and deteriorating conditions of service during the early 1930s – for many only the observance of their 'well-earned rights' had reconciled them to the Republic at all (see Document 52). The membership rolls of the NSDAP and SA include a significant cohort of activists from this new middle class and Jürgen Falter's definitive study of the Nazi electorate concludes that some voted NSDAP, although they were not dis-proportionately inclined to do so.[15]

III

There remains the question of why this diverse middle-class constituency should have been attracted specifically to Nazism rather than to another anti-republican party. It was suggested earlier (in Chapter 2) that the National Socialists were singularly successful in exploiting the powerful *völkisch*-nationalist senti-ments which pervaded inter-war Germany and of which they themselves were a product. These sentiments were widespread in middle-class circles and notions of national community and national ethnic solidarity surface repeatedly in the writings of middle-class Nazis (see Document 18). As will be seen in due course, this same *völkisch* nationalism also allowed these middle-class supporters to reconcile their adherence to National Socialism with other facets of the movement which have been neglected by or unknown to historians until very recently.

Beyond the *völkisch* dimension, a range of influential studies, such as Heinrich-August Winkler's *Mittelstand Demokratie und Nationalsozialismus*,[16] have confirmed the strength of authoritarian, anti-parliamentarian and anti-modernist inclinations within Germany's middle classes which left the Weimar Republic – purportedly a 'bourgeois democracy' – with relatively few bourgeois supporters. As Kurt Sontheimer has exclaimed: 'How can a democracy exist without democrats?'[17] The origins of the problem predate Weimar's tenuous existence. Historians of nineteenth- and even eighteenth-century Germany have often written with at least half an eye inclined towards the National Socialist disaster of the twentieth century. At the heart of the matter was the perceived failure of German liberalism to seize control of high politics and remould the constitution on parliamentarian lines, most notably in 1848–49 or during the

1860s, despite the rapid industrialisation and urbanisation of the mid and later nineteenth century. Looked at differently, a monarchist, aristocratic and authoritarian form of government prevailed in Germany up until 1918 in spite of decades of socio-economic modernisation, leaving the middle classes without any tradition or experience of political responsibility at national level. With Britain's record of concurrent industrialisation and liberalisation taken to be 'normal', Germany's history was said to have taken a special path or *Sonderweg*: a phenomenon often viewed positively by the right, but negatively by the left who have seen within this special path the seeds of Nazism. In David Blackbourn's words, this latter school of thought points to 'the failure of the bourgeoisie to conduct itself like a "proper" bourgeoisie', which would have created a parliamentary political order to govern industrial society.[18]

Blackbourn himself has been instrumental in creating a more nuanced picture of middle-class politics in imperial Germany, paying particular attention to the role of the bourgeoisie in civil society. He freely accepts that the middle classes played a very limited prescriptive role in high politics, but argues that rather than 'taking the money and running', the bourgeoisie could regard the Civil Code of 1900 as the enactment of their social ideals. Furthermore, he observes, guaranteed legal freedoms and an accountable bureaucracy were significant bourgeois achievements, and a wide range of bourgeois voluntary associations came to influence many areas of public life. That said, the weakness of the bourgeoisie in national politics and more specifically the weakness of the National Liberals in Parliament did create a particular set of problems as the masses – working-class, lower middle-class or peasantry – entered the political stage. The result was conflict as the Social Democrats made gains, in response to which non-socialist groups, including the aristocracy, sought to mobilise lower middle-class support and retain an element of working-class backing by resorting to rhetoric and strident demagogy. Unable to project power at national level, 'bourgeois liberalism saw many of its worst fears realised as it became the most palpable victim of the vigorous mass politics at the end of the century, wedged between the SPD on the left and a rejuvenated popularized right'. As lower middle-class demands were accommodated in this demagogic way, but as any attempts at fundamental reform failed, a political climate was created in which the Nazis' later success became thinkable.[19] In this context it is significant that although the National Socialists themselves were highly accomplished in the use of strident demagogy, their declared aims included elimination of this domestic political conflict, which the bourgeoisie abhorred, and the restoration of social harmony, which the lower middle classes also demanded.

It therefore seems clear that an understanding of the middle classes' role in the rise of Nazism must include consideration of the upper middle classes as well as the petty bourgeoisie. Empirical research into the social background of the Nazis' members and voters has underlined the need for this broader approach. Many younger, aspiring members of upper middle-class society, including university students and newly qualified professionals, were active in the movement, while in Protestant towns and cities, upper middle-class districts often voted in strength for the Nazis. The characterisation of National Socialism as a particularly wide-reaching middle-class *rassemblement* has, therefore, attracted broad support recently among historians in Germany and elsewhere. Different elements of the middle classes had come to Nazism for a variety of conflicting reasons, and even in fear of each other, but anticipated that Hitler would succeed in imposing the political, social and economic quietude on their turbulent country for which they all yearned. The political alternatives were either too hidebound in their old, sectarian patterns of behaviour or exerted too narrow an appeal to be credible in this regard.

Clearly, then, the pattern of developments at national level goes a long way towards explaining the attraction National Socialism held for many Germans. It offered all sections of the middle classes the prospect of a coherence and cohesion which bourgeois politics had hitherto lacked (see Documents 10, 20–22). However, Nazi fortunes at national level were intertwined with those at local or regional level, and here the reasons for Hitler's breakthrough require further expanation. Although bourgeois politics appeared relatively ineffectual at national level, middle-class institutional and political life at local level remained more robust, and the grandees and notables who set the tone of local political life were not at the outset Nazis. How would local Nazis and Nazi organisations penetrate or over-whelm these existing networks?

IV

During the later 1920s there was certainly growing disillu-sionment at regional and local level with parliamentary parties which had been expected to represent at the centre specific material interests or regional particularist aspirations. The DNVP, for example, had enjoyed close links with Protestant farming associations such as the National Rural League (*Reichslandbund*), but the latter particularly resented the DNVP's participation in Weimar governments which could not be accused of especially favouring agriculture. The next step was to turn to agrarian special interest parties which polled well in 1928 and 1930, but they were quite unequal to resolving the severe economic problems of the early 1930s, despite the high expecta-tions they had created. It was in this context that the NSDAP's vigorous agrarian campaign, launched in 1930, proved effective (see Documents 48–51). Within the framework of their *völkisch* programme, the National Socialists were able to convince sub-stantial parts of the farming community that although their sec-tional interests could not be realised in relative isolation, farming would be accorded its rightful place within a new, national com-munity. Within this context farming was promised a package of financial and legislative assistance, including a high external tariff on agricultural goods. If there were to be no outright winners within the national ethnic community in the Nazi scheme of things, there were to be no outright losers either.

The small businessmen, independent craftsmen, public employees and salaried staff of Weimar Germany suffered their share of material difficulties during the Depression, but most local histories agree that their economic problems were less deep-seated than those of agriculture. Many individual middle-class citizens were even able to build up their bank deposits during these years. However, the local networks of leagues, associations and pressure groups proved ominously fragile within the national Weimar system, where mass politics were legitimised and actively practised by the Social Democrats in particular. Craftsmen discovered that their workforces, regarded by them as members of the local guild community, were perceived by trade union and Social Democratic officials as potential members of the national labour movement. And if the middle classes were not the main victims of the Great Depression, they none the less discovered that their traditional way of conducting politics offered little protection and no prospect of attaining longer-term objectives. The wider German crisis left deepening psychological and political wounds. The middle classes did not suffer much unemployment themselves (but see Document 54), but they feared the consequences for their own futures of other people's unemployment; not least as tensions with local Social Democrats and Communists sharpened and the threat of physical violence hung over the towns and provinces of Germany. A series of local histories have traced the Nazis' success in mobilising a significant proportion of this disoriented middle class behind the banner of a communal and national solidarity which, if it excluded the socialist working class, seemed to embrace almost everyone else (see Documents 48–52).

It would be an exaggeration to suggest that an unqualified Nazification of the (Protestant) middle classes occurred. Local bourgeois clubs and associations retained their identity often beyond the end of Weimar, and important national organisations, such as the nationalist white-collar union, the DHV, or the monarchist paramilitary league, the Stahlhelm, maintained a distinctive existence at local and regional level (see Documents 5, 53). Similarly, agrarian associations such as the *Reichslandbund* continued to operate. The evidence suggests that while Protestant farmers eventually voted Nazi in droves, smaller numbers actually joined the party or the SA, and this equivocal pattern of behaviour typified the middle-class response to National Socialism. However, the older middle-class associations either wished or felt constrained to adopt a political vocabulary and outlook similar to, or at least compatible with that of Nazism. This not only assisted the further advance of National Socialism, but also makes it slightly misleading to regard the 37.4 per cent poll achieved by the Nazis in July 1932, or the 43.9 per cent of March 1933, as definitive high tide marks. There were many Germans who, if not themselves Nazi activists or voters, were still happy enough to hand the National Socialists the keys to the front door.

The NSDAP itself appears to have understood this well. As

was shown in Chapter 4, Hitler insisted that Nazi organisations retain their distinctiveness and integrity. Dual membership of a National Socialist organisation and any non-Nazi counterpart was not permitted in theory and eventually seldom tolerated in practice. However, the Nazis were not averse to co-operating with other 'nationally minded' parties or organisations where no better choice offered itself. Nazi participation in the anti-Young Plan campaign or the Harzburg Front were examples at national level; the modus operandi of Darré's Agricultural Affairs Bureau (*Agrarpolitischer Apparat*) was an excellent example of the same at local level. Darré did not seek to disrupt or displace existing agrarian organisations, but instead provided for the training of speakers and activists capable of infiltrating them from below in order, as Gustavo Corni puts it, 'to produce a mass concensus which would serve as a means of pressurising the old ruling elites'.[20] There were comparable developments in the towns and cities of Germany as Nazis appeared individually or severally in State Parliaments, town councils, school boards, trade associations, clubs and societies – sometimes achieving control, sometimes not – yet simultaneously developed where possible parallel Nazi organisations which were intended to dominate their particular area of institutional life in the future Third Reich.

The vital and glaring exception to this pattern occurred in the Catholic parts of Germany, which contained about a third of the population. Here corporate life in general was less receptive to National Socialism and although politics displayed increasingly authoritarian, anti-republican traits, they did so with a Catholic rather than a Nazi accent (see Document 4). John Conway assesses that the attitude of the clergy towards Nazism, which obviously did much to shape the political outlook of Catholic congregations, ranged from hostile to reserved. However, although Nazism's racialist doctrines were rejected outright, a certain sympathy with its anti-Marxist and especially its anti-communist stance was present.[21] Thus middle-class Catholic Germany was not immune to Nazism. Success was harder to achieve, but as Oded Heilbronner has recently demonstrated, it was possible in circumstances where local corporative life had degenerated sufficiently to leave organisational space which the National Socialists could fill.[22] That said, the partial Nazification of middle-class institutional life which occurred in much of

Protestant Germany, where many individual church ministers were enthusiastic supporters of the NSDAP, was not matched in the Catholic areas. Voting figures give an indication of this contrast in Nazi fortunes. In July 1932 some 38 per cent of registered Protestant voters supported the Nazis, but just 16 per cent of registered Catholic voters.

V

An impressive body of evidence, therefore, supports the overall picture of National Socialism as a predominantly Protestant, middle-class *rassemblement*, and this line of interpretation has provided the starting point and the conclusion for most of the recent general histories of Nazism. Few historians would claim that the Nazi movement was monolithically middle-class, for the presence of working-class voters and activists has always been acknowledged. However, their numbers have been regarded as too small to affect the prevailing, middle-class explanatory model. The latest empirical work on the National Socialist constituency has now created problems for this long-standing consensus which have yet to be fully addressed. It appears that some 40 per cent of voters and party members and some 60 per cent of SA members were working-class, leading to the typification of Nazism as a popular or people's movement instead of a class movement (see Documents 45–47). The social and political breadth of the Nazi constituency was underlined by its ability to attract a substantial proportion of its working-class voters from the Social Democratic and even the Communist camp. Furthermore by July 1932, Jürgen Falter observes, the NSDAP's working-class electorate apparently was larger in absolute terms than either the SPD or KPD received in that Reichstag election.[23] This startling claim inevitably raises afresh the question of what, precisely, motivated middle-class Germans to turn to Nazism if so many of its supporters were purportedly their class enemies.

The problem is accentuated if we consider the social make-up of National Socialism in its Protestant rural and small-town strongholds, for it was precisely here that its working-class support tended to peak and yet precisely in local histories of such areas that the picture of Nazism as a middle-class movement has emerged most persuasively. Lower Saxony is an excellent case in point. It has provided the focus for several outstanding studies, all of which emphasise the middle-class, anti-Social Democratic character of the NSDAP in this Protestant region of north-western Germany. However, Detlef Mühlberger's recent sociological study of the Nazi movement's membership poses problems for parts of this interpretation. His book includes consideration of the party *Gau* South-Hanover-Brunswick which lay within Lower Saxony and also Lower Saxon SA units from Groß Ilsede and Northeim County and concludes that over the years 1925 to 1933 the NSDAP in this *Gau* was around 60 per cent middle-class and 40 per cent working-class, if members whose status was unclear are eliminated from the picture (see Document 45). The Nazi party in South-Hanover-Brunswick certainly attracted a disproportionate number of middle-class members, but also a sufficiently creditable tally of workers to prevent its characterisation as 'middle-class'. If the recruitment figures are examined on a year-by-year basis this conclusion is reinforced for the early 1930s in particular, since the proportion of workers among new recruits whose socal status was clear rose each year to peak at 42.8 per cent in 1932.[24] It appears that as the Depression ravaged the region and political tensions grew, almost as many workers joined the Nazi party as did middle-class citizens.

Consideration of individual party branches in the *Gau* prejudices still further the old orthodoxy of the Lower Saxon NSDAP as a party with a pronounced class profile. Of the seventeen branches Mühlberger has examined, five were over three-quarters middle-class, two were over two-thirds working-class, but the remaining ten were socially mixed. Farmers, salesmen, students and white-collar staff coexisted with workers, some agricultural but most not, in the same branches. Thus the typical Nazi party branch in South-Hanover-Brunswick had middle- and working-class members present in strength.[25] The two SA units were overwhelmingly working-class.[26] The unit from Northeim County was, fortuitously, one of those which featured in William Sheridan Allen's famous history of the town of Northeim (under the pseudonym of Thalburg). The best information then available led him to write of an SA 'composed largely of farmers' sons' and hence, it appeared, the physical expression of middle-class political militancy.[27] In fact 88.6 per cent of the unit's members were workers, within which total just 11.4 per cent were identified as agricultural labourers.[28]

It appears that the irresistable force of a socially heterogeneous Nazi movement has met with the immovable object of a meticulously researched literature which emphasises the middle-class basis of Nazism. Peter Fritzsche's history of Lower Saxony – in which he characterises Nazism as an 'antisocialist bourgeois union of impressive proportions' – is a notable recent addition.[29] There is clearly a need for historians to square this awkward circle. Of course much of the evidence and many of the arguments discussed above are in no need of revision. The contention that the middle classes suffered in a variety of ways during the Weimar era and that many opposed or came to oppose the Republic and its Social Democratic guardians appears eminently sound. The SPD's advocacy of collective working-class interests and the trade unions' representation of collective employee interests also threatened and angered many middle-class Germans. That middle-class politics slid into crisis is also indisputable, and the benefits for the Nazi movement once the limitations of interest group politics became apparent were manifest. However, it might be that the National Socialists attracted their middle-class constituency not because they promised to rally it against the workers, but because they strove to short-circuit the language of class politics altogether through their advocacy of the national ethnic community.

The existing literature on the Lower Saxon Nazi movement provides ample evidence to support this contention if the regional NSDAP is regarded as socially amorphous and not, as traditionally believed, overwhelmingly middle-class. Thus the language of cohesion and national solidarity is cited repeatedly by Allen. His examples include a pastor who likened the NSDAP to the imperial army because 'both represented the whole of the German people and not any specific group',[30] the Hitler Youth veteran who subsequently praised that organisation because 'there were no social or class distinctions',[31] or the prosperous businessman who recounted that he and his wife 'believed the common people should have a better life and that socialism was essential. We were idealists. In fact we were among the few people who had something to lose, for my business was successful'.[32]

Similarly Noakes observes that the NSDAP gained a mass

following across Lower Saxony through its advocacy of the *Volksgemeinschaft*, its attacks on the divisive party system, and its activism, all of which distinguished it from the conventional right.[33] He also emphasises the 'classlessness of [the NSDAP's] organisation', which again set it apart from the other parties.[34] Noakes concluded in 1971 that this process of integration involved the middle classes of the region, to the virtual exclusion of the workers.[35] However, in the light of the newest evidence, it appears that the middle-class sentiments cited by Allen, advocating an end to class conflict, can be taken more literally than once believed. Similarly the NSDAP's integrative capacities observed by Noakes were not confined to the middle classes, although that in itself was a prodigious achievement, but instead cut across class barriers in unprecedented fashion to include workers. Thomas Childers writes of the NSDAP's ability to speak 'the language of both transcendent class or even national solidarity *and* sectarian special interest',[36] and it does indeed appear that many middle-class Nazis did not seek to regroup around the banner of special interest politics or class warfare, instead seeking an escape from them. Not only were they weary of such struggle, but feared its consequences if it continued unchecked and ended in a Social Democratic, or still worse a Communist, victory. By integrating people from all walks of life the Nazis offered these middle-class followers the prospect of a political and social truce once the 'classless' National Socialist movement had overthrown Weimar and remoulded society in its own image. As it happened, events after January 1933 were not so straightforward. The degree of success the Nazis had in achieving their social objectives remains highly questionable, but until Hitler's takeover middle- and working-class Germans co-operated to overthrow a constitution and system of values on which they blamed their country's problems and their own fears and suffering.

Notes

1 Frank Domurad, 'The Politics of Corporatism: Hamburg Handicraft in the late Weimar Republic, 1927–1933', in Richard Bessel and E. J. Feuchtwanger (eds.), *Social Change and Political Development in Weimar Germany*, London, Totowa, NJ, 1981, p. 188.

2 Jeremy Noakes, *The Nazi Party in Lower Saxony 1921–1933*, Oxford,

1971, pp. 118–19.

3 Larry Eugene Jones, 'The Dissolution of the Bourgeois Party System in the Weimar Republic', in Bessel and Feuchtwanger (eds.), *Weimar Germany*, p. 275.

4 Thomas Childers, 'The middle classes and National Socialism', in David Blackbourn and Richard J. Evans (eds.), *The German Bourgeoisie*, London, New York, 1991, p. 326.

5 Karl Dietrich Bracher, *The German Dictatorship. The Origins, Structure and Effects of National Socialism*, trans. J. Steinberg, London, 1973, p. 145; first publ. 1969.

6 Hans Mommsen, *Die verspielte Freiheit. Der Weg der Republik von Weimar in den Untergang 1918 bis 1933*, Frankfurt-am-Main, Berlin, 1990, p. 321.

7 Quoted in Jane Degras (ed.), *The Communist International 1919–1943. Documents*, London, 1971, vol. i, p. 12.

8 Quoted in Heinrich-August Winkler, *Von der Revolution zur Stabilisierung. Arbeiter und Arbeiterbewegung in der Weimarer Republik 1918 bis 1924*, Berlin, Bonn, 1984, p. 582.

9 Paraphrased in Martin Kitchen, *Fascism*, London, 1976, p. 66.

10 Paraphrased in Kitchen, *Fascism*, p. 60.

11 Talcott Parsons, *Essays in Sociological Theory*, New York, 1949. Seymour Martin Lipset, *Political Man. The Social Bases of Politics*, Baltimore, 1981; first published 1959.

12 Lipset, *Political Man*, p. 148.

13 Francis L. Carsten, *The Rise of Fascism*, London, 1967, p. 233.

14 Theodor Geiger, *Die Klassengesellschaft im Schmelztiegel*, Cologne, Hagen, 1949, pp. 57–73, 168–76; Ludwig Preller, *Sozialpolitik in der Weimarer Republik*, Düsseldorf, 1978, pp. 99–100.

15 Jürgen W. Falter, *Hitlers Wähler*, Munich, 1991, pp. 230 ff, 242 ff.

16 Heinrich-August Winkler, *Mittelstand Demokratie und Nationalsozialismus. Die politische Entwicklung von Handwerk und Kleinhandel in der Weimarer Republik*, Cologne, 1972.

17 Kurt Sontheimer, 'The Weimar Republic – Failure and Prospects of German Democracy', in E. J. Feuchtwanger (ed.), *Upheaval and Continuity. A Century of German History*, London, 1973, p. 101.

18 David Blackbourn and Geoff Eley, *The Peculiarities of German History. Bourgeois Society and Politics in Nineteenth-Century Germany*, Oxford, New York, 1984, p. 287.

19 David Blackbourn, 'The Discreet Charm of the Bourgeoisie: Some Recent Works on German History', *European Studies Review*, 11, 1981, p. 252.

20 Gustavo Corni, 'Richard Walther Darré: The Blood and Iron Ideologue', in Ronald Smelser and Rainer Zitelmann (eds.), *The Nazi Elite*, trans. M. Fischer, Basingstoke, London, 1993, p. 20.

21   John S. Conway, 'National Socialism and the Christian Churches during the Weimar Republic', in Peter D. Stachura (ed.), *The Nazi Machtergreifung*, London, Boston, Sydney, 1983, esp. pp. 136–7.

22   Oded Heilbronner, 'Der verlassene Stammtisch. Vom Verfall der bürgerlichen Infrastruktur und dem Aufstieg der NSDAP am Beispiel der Region Schwarzwald', *Geschichte und Gesellschaft*, 19, 1993, pp. 178–201.

23   Falter, *Wähler*, p. 225.

24   Detlef Mühlberger, *Hitler's Followers*, London, 1990, ch. 5.

25   *Ibid.*, ch. 5.

26   *Ibid.*, table 6.1.

27   William Sheridan Allen, *The Nazi Seizure of Power. The Experience of a Single German Town 1930–1935*, London, 1966, p. 75.

28   See note 26 above.

29   Peter Fritzsche, *Rehearsals for Fascism. Populism and Political Mobilisation in Weimar Germany*, New York, Oxford, 1990, p. 235.

30   Allen, *Nazi Seizure*, p. 40.

31   *Ibid.*, p. 73.

32   *Ibid.*, p. 77.

33   Noakes, *Nazi Party*, p. 125.

34   *Ibid.*, p. 220.

35   *Ibid.*, pp. 248–9.

36   Childers, 'Middle Classes', p. 330.

6

The formation of the Nazi constituency: the working classes

I

The history of Germany's middle classes appears to explain their attraction to Nazism, but the history of the working classes appears to show why they should not have turned to the Nazis. German working-class politicians were able to build up a mass party, the SPD, with the potential to dominate national politics, and trade unionists merely awaited a change in the constitutional and legal climate to enable them to become pre-eminent in labour politics in the workplace. When, in November 1918, the last imperial Chancellor, Prince Max von Baden, handed the SPD the keys to Germany's political future, working-class politics appeared to have come of age. In the event the Social Democrats and official trade unions chose to work with and within the existing socio-economic order, but important constitutional and welfare reforms were achieved and in 1928 the SPD remained the largest party in Germany with around a million members and almost a third of the vote. That said, the harsh peace settlement, civil war and economic turmoil all took their toll of the Social Democrats' self-confidence and popularity. However, these difficulties apparently turned some 10 per cent of the electorate towards the Communist Party and not towards the Nazis at all. With many Catholic workers backing the Centre Party, there seemed little working-class support left for the National Socialists to glean. While the previous chapter on the middle classes could only skim over a substantial and distinguished literature, this chapter is, consequently, confronted in quantitative terms by more meagre fare.

In fact more has been written over the years on why workers did not support the Nazis. It has been claimed that the National Socialists themselves, having tried and failed to woo the workers in the 1928 elections, then abandoned these tactics and turned instead to the lower middle classes where rich pickings were to be had. The non-appearance of workers at meetings, the dearth of working-class electoral support and the relative lack of working-class members in the party and its ancillary organisations appeared to be the inevitable corollary of this new strategy. Martin Broszat was prominent among historians who around 1980 began to doubt whether the Nazis' espousal of a middle-class strategy had really been so single-minded,[1] but the most serious doubts began to creep in as membership records were subjected to intense scrutiny from the 1970s onward and computer technology allowed new insights into the make-up of the Nazi electorate.

Before this the only detailed evidence for the composition of the Nazi Party nationally had been compiled by the NSDAP itself and was published in 1935. It suggested that around a quarter of party members in September 1930 were workers, under a third in January 1933 and about 30 per cent in January 1935.[2] Historians argued that the figures were probably unreliable and that, through wishful thinking and thanks to idiosyncratic Nazi definition of the term 'worker', they probably exaggerated the working-class presence in the party. In any case, since almost half the overall population was working-class, the workers were apparently clearly underrepresented in the Nazi movement and little more was said about them.

The electoral evidence seemed to suggest that an even smaller proportion of Nazi voters were workers. The two large Marxist parties in Germany, the republican SPD and the revolutionary KPD, saw their aggregate vote remain remarkably stable during the final years of Weimar, although their combined percentage share of the vote did fall slightly. As seen previously, the 'middle-class' parties fared very much worse. Many collapsed almost entirely – including various interest group parties which represented farming, small business or regional interests – and even the conservative DNVP lost more than half its electoral support. The only real exception to this was the ability of the Catholic Centre Party and its Bavarian affiliate, the BVP, to maintain their absolute vote at least up to and including November 1932. It was therefore concluded that the Protestant middle-class, particularly the lower middle-class, electorate had played a disproportionate part in the electoral rise of the NSDAP.

Recent research on the social composition of the Nazi movement's membership and electorate indicates that this interpretation was erroneous in certain key respects. The Nazi Party membership records and those of affiliated organisations such as the Storm-troopers (SA) which began to be discovered in German archives during the 1970s were, and remain, of varying quality, but it has been possible to establish from them the sociology of many individual party branches, SA and SS units or sometimes recruitment patterns in particular towns or regions over a year or more. Information concerning occupation, age, sex, and sometimes factors such as marital status, employment record, parental background and the like became available, and by the early 1990s the weight of evidence indicated that the NSDAP nationally contained a substantial working-class element. Some individual party branches, in a wide variety of social and economic settings, were largely working-class while ancillary organisations nationally were often more working-class than middle-class. The most recent research findings suggest that during the Weimar era slightly over 40 per cent of Nazi Party members were from a working-class background (see Document 45). Similar studies confirm earlier estimates that the SA's membership was 60 per cent or more working-class (see Document 46), and it appears that even the elite SS recruited about half its rank and file from the working classes. Historians have also paid greater attention to the National Socialist labour organisation, the NSBO, which, with around 300,000 members, had grown larger than its Communist counterpart before the end of Weimar. However, precise figures on the respective proportions of blue- and white-collar employees within the NSBO remain unavailable.

The question arises of why the NSDAP's own membership survey, the *Partei-Statistik* of 1935, showed a working-class presence of around only 30 per cent in January 1933 and January 1935 and rather less than this in September 1930. The answer is provided by the techniques used in this survey. Party officials concerned requested from each party district meticulously accurate information on its membership as of 1 January 1935; entries made for 30 September 1930 and 31 January 1933 only included 1935 members who had joined at the earlier dates. Therefore members who had joined earlier, but had then left the party before 1935 were lost from view. Workers found the payment of a monthly 1RM due to the party a considerable financial burden and this was undoubtedly one reason for a higher rate of turnover among working-class party members. It should be noted that the Communist Party had had even greater problems in this regard. Only with the recent re-examination of actual membership records has it become clear that at any one time in the period up to 1933 the NSDAP's membership was, as noted, around 40 per cent working-class.

The most recent electoral studies have come to similar conclusions. In the early 1980s the use of computers in historical research allowed electoral historians to compile, collate and interpret enormous quantities of statistical data and, through the use of a range of analytical techniques such as multivariate regression analysis and contrast group analysis, they began to uncover the complex relationships which existed between social background and voting behaviour. The pioneering studies were not without their methodological problems, but their tendency to stress the eclecticism of National Socialism's electoral appeal has, recently, been not only confirmed but underlined. In the past few years comprehensive examination of Weimar election results has indicated that a good 40 per cent of the NSDAP's voters were working-class, remarkably similar to the proportion of workers in the party itself (see Document 47). Looked at differently this meant that one worker in three was voting Nazi by March 1933, and that some 200,000 or more had joined the NSDAP, some 300,000 (most not simultaneously in the party) the SA, and a sizable number the NSBO by the end of 1932. A conservative estimate would have to conclude that at least 500,000 workers belonged to Nazi organisations during 1932.

II

Few, if any, historians would now contest the general validity of these findings, but there has been a lively debate in recent years over who, precisely, these working-class Nazis were. The issue centres on the acknowledged diversity of lifestyles and political loyalties within the working classes. A farm labourer working on a large estate in the north-east of the country was a far cry from the shipwright in Bremen or steelworker in Essen. The coalminers of the Ruhr District had little, if anything, in common with Thuringian or Saxon women who made lacewear or other high-value products in their own homes in a manner reminiscent of the pre-industrial putting-out system. Workers in large engineering plants or chemical works lived very different lives from employees in small firms who worked closely with their bosses, often within the ethos of the guild economy. Even within large-scale industry, levels of skill and the extent of a craft ethos varied widely, and on top of these distinctions religion, national origins and regional identity were all of considerable importance. Within the Ruhr District, for example, Catholic communities delivered a large working-class vote to the Centre Party, although many such voters switched to the KPD during the Depression. Many Protestant workers voted National Liberal before 1914 or even DNVP, feeling that they were part of mainstream (Protestant) German society in a way that the Catholics (often Polish-speaking or Italian migrants) were not. The SPD only became dominant in Ruhr politics some years after the Second World War. All in all it is estimated that the SPD and KPD together received about half the working-class vote during the Weimar era, and any attempt simply to equate working-class politics with Marxist politics is widely recognised as being too simplistic.

Turning first to the electoral question, it has, therefore, been argued that there were plenty of working-class votes to be won without necessarily competing against the Marxist parties for support. The evidence does suggest that the NSDAP polled best in areas where craft workers, agricultural labourers and employees in small- and medium-scale industry predominated. The NSDAP also polled reasonably in industrial regions, but here a German equivalent of the British 'Tory' working-class ethos has been evoked. As noted, many Protestant workers in the Ruhr Valley had habitually voted National Liberal through an identification with the (Protestant) national State and with the employer paternalism which was widespread there. Company housing (often of a good standard), promotion and greater job security were the anticipated and often the actual rewards. Similarly, many younger Ruhr workers in particular joined the monarchist paramilitary league, the Stahlhelm, whether in order to advance their careers or because they genuinely subscribed to its militarist and monarchist values. In other words the NSDAP had an ample pool of working-class support to draw upon, whose members shared aspects of their lifestyle or their politics with the middle classes. If they were, indeed, the bedrock of working-class Nazism then it could be argued that precisely because of their middle-class affinities, these workers found the NSDAP an attractive radical option during the early 1930s.

However, recent electoral studies indicate that the National Socialists probably gained support from most types of worker and not just peripheral groups, as the non-Marxists are sometimes called. Here it should be stressed that the NSDAP was keen on maximising its constituency and was at pains to recruit 'Tory' workers, but strove equally to attract former Social Democrats and Communists, and also Catholic workers. Of the major parties in late Weimar Germany, the NSDAP was distinguished by its ability (and the need) to mobilise an electoral constituency more or less from scratch. Almost all of its supporters in September 1930 had not backed the party in a previous election, and by July 1932 13 million voters supported the Nazis who had not done so before 1930. Jürgen Falter has demonstrated that first-time voters, previous abstainers and particularly defectors from other parties all played a part in this process and the 40 per cent of Nazi voters who were working-class were no different in this regard.[3] Of those who had previously voted for other parties, about half were erstwhile 'Marxist' voters of whom the majority were former Social Democrats. Falter estimates that the SPD saw three million of its supporters switch to the NSDAP between 1930 and 1933 (although it gained one million voters from the NSDAP by way of compensation), and there is now evidence to suggest that the NSDAP did significantly better than the Communist Party in attracting radicalised Social Democratic voters during this period. Over the same timespan more than half a million voters deserted the KPD for the NSDAP.[4] The political background of Nazi working-class voters (roughly 50 per cent ex-Marxist, 50 per cent non-Marxist) was, therefore, comparable with the political background of the working class as a whole, which is what one might expect if the NSDAP was, indeed, a 'people's' or integration party.

Turning to working-class members of Nazi organisations, Detlef Mühlberger's findings indicate a diverse range of social backgrounds, albeit with an overwhelming preponderance of non-agricultural workers and within that a clear majority of the skilled workers who were the bedrock of Germany's working class and of the SPD. That said, the NSDAP's working-class membership had a more rural and small-town flavour than did the SPD's, although the distinction was by no means absolute.[5] A comprehensive study of the NSDAP's younger membership by Falter confirms Mühlberger's regionally based conclusions. Employees from manufacturing and industry constituted the bedrock of the NSDAP's younger working-class membership and the moderate under-representation of workers which did occur resulted from a failure to recruit many agricultural workers.[6] Recent work by William Brustein suggests that an astonishing 50 per cent of working-class Nazis were engaged in the staples sector, metallurgy and mining.[7] The SA's working-class membership was younger, but again included few agricultural labourers and a majority of skilled workers (see Document 46). Most were unemployed and this, along with their youth, suggests comparison with the KPD's membership rather than that of the SPD.

All in all the National Socialist Party contained a significantly higher number of workers among its voters and activists than was once believed. A proportion of 40 per cent has now become widely accepted. Had the Nazi Party's social make-up reflected that of German society perfectly the figure would have been even higher, but the most obviously under-represented part of society within the party is better defined in gender than in class terms. Women were seldom party members, nor did they receive much encouragement to join. Furthermore what under-representation of workers there was within the party was offset quite significantly by the SA's ability to recruit a much higher proportion of workers, some 60 per cent, to its ranks.

III

This raises questions concerning the precise nature of the appeal National Socialism exerted within the working class but, unfortunately, there are no particularly straightforward answers available. It is possible to detect specifically working-class motivation, with factors such as job creation and frustration with existing working-class parties being cases in point (of which more later), but there were also forces at work which were less obviously related to class politics.

Richard Hamilton noted some years ago that entire rural communities in Protestant northern Germany were voting National Socialist by 1932.[8] This observation was intended to undermine the notion that the Nazi breakthrough in that part of Germany was a specifically lower middle-class affair, suggesting instead that these communities had turned to the NSDAP as communities *per se* and not through a set of interests specific to a single class. However, by the same token the working-class members of these communities must, if Hamilton's hypothesis is correct, also have supported the Nazis for reasons of communal solidarity. The same might conceivably hold for the very substantial proportion of party members and storm-troopers from a working-class background whom Mühlberger has found in the NSDAP and SA pre-1933 membership records for rural Lower Saxony.[9] If class rather than communal interests had, indeed, drawn both the lower middle and working classes of the rural north into the Nazi movement, then one would be hard put to explain precisely how these apparent class enemies managed to coexist within the same party branches and SA units. The communal explanation appears more convincing and may not have been restricted solely to the countryside. Ingrid Buchloh in her study of the NSDAP in Duisburg identified support for the National Socialists from most sections of the community and argues that the NSDAP was able to construct its heterogeneous constituency precisely by appealing to factors which transcended the class divide. Small businesses, for example, were urged to recognise that the closure of the Ruhrort-Meiderich steelworks would impoverish their working-class customers while the workers themselves were told that the community would have to sink or swim together.[10]

Community also affected the National Socialist movement's prospects in another way. The entire movement was organised on militarist lines with chains of command which resembled those of a wartime army, added to which was a party and SA ethos which owed a great deal to the memory of the 'Front Community' (see Documents 17, 18). The predominantly middle-class leaders of the movement were frequently war veterans who had commanded (working-class) troops and could therefore relate to working-class colleagues within a militarised organisational framework, emphasised all the more by the wearing of uniforms. Workers from the war generation had also been made familiar with their subordinate role within this context, where in the SA the leading role accorded to middle-class leaders was compensated for by the espousal of solidarity and common cause by the entire movement, again with reference to the wartime experience. Even younger workers who had not seen military service had none the less grown up within an environment where such militarist and *völkisch* values were prominent. In this regard the strongly working-class SA could be seen almost as an outgrowth of the wartime army, albeit encompassing the post-war generation.

Leaving aside the question of communal solidarity for the moment, aspects of the National Socialist movement's social profile, such as age and unemployment, were also likely to boost the size of its working-class constituency. It is generally accepted that the National Socialist movement was relatively youthful and its paramilitary auxiliary, the SA, accentuated this tendency by recruiting its rank-and-file membership from the 18 to 35 age range, although SA reservists could be older. The German census shows that a very high proportion of young, economically active Germans were in occupations categorised as working-class; with age came promotion, the acquisition of additional skills or the acquisition of independent status by some skilled workers. In other words, any appeal by the Nazi movement to youth would, all else being equal, provide a constituency which was strongly working-class.

The unemployment question is rather less straightforward since it is acknowledged that the NSDAP fared markedly less well than the Communist Party in attracting votes from the unemployed during the early 1930s. Furthermore, it appears that the NSDAP did proportionately better among white-collar unemployed voters than among the working-class unemployed. Falter estimates that in July 1932 just 13 per cent of unemployed workers voted NSDAP whilst 29 per cent voted Communist.[11]

However the SA, with a membership of 450,000 in mid 1932, recruited predominantly from the young male unemployed. These three social categories – youth, males and the unemployed – are all associated positively, to varying degrees, with the working class. A higher proportion of the young working popu- lation was classified as working-class than was the old, a higher proportion of the male working population was classified as working-class than was the female, and in particular a far higher proportion of the unemployed population was working-class than was lower middle-class. In a sense, therefore, it could be argued that regardless of the class appeal of National Socialism, if it attracted young male unemployed recruits into the SA, then it would, unavoidably, attract many workers.

That said, it is equally possible to detect concerns, aspirations or ideals integral to the working classes which attracted some workers to National Socialism. Starting again with the unem- ployed membership of the SA, it is notable that skilled workers predominated. Many of the SA's recruits had been asked to write a curriculum vitae or provide a written account of their reasons for joining; and from those which have survived it is possible to discern a widespread sense of outrage among the skilled working-class recruits that their training and skills suddenly counted for nothing, that the relatively secure existence and relatively interesting work they had expected to obtain or retain had disappeared in the slump. Idleness, hunger and the poverty and suffering of many friends and family members, the meagreness of social security provision for young, single men and the apparent powerlessness of the Social Democratic Party and trade unions either to prevent or resolve the catastrophe alienated many of these young workers from the traditional labour movement (see Documents 59–61). The Communist movement proved one vehicle of protest, but the National Socialist movement combined protest with the provision of basic material assistance and the promise of rapid, concrete measures to revive the labour market once in power. The material assis- tance itself was the result of door-to-door collections from better- off members and sympathisers or the collection of food from farmers and peasants who were unable to find a market for all their produce. In this way some amelioration of working-class poverty was achieved through a rudimentary form of the national ethnic community which the NSDAP advocated (see Documents 38–40, 43, 44).

Looking at the NSDAP's broader working-class constituency, it appears from electoral surveys that employed rather than unemployed workers were more supportive of the Nazi Party at the polls. Similarly the working-class membership of the party, and especially the NSBO, was by no means predominantly unemployed. Given that skilled and semi-skilled workers (the majority of the working class in Germany) were strongly in evidence, Eve Rosenhaft's observation that in Berlin those workers who perceived themselves as 'respectable' were prominent among the NSDAP's working-class support appears highly plausible. The Nazis stressed the need to return to times of stability, or normalcy, which appealed as much to working-class women, exasperated at having to put up with their idle menfolk cluttering up the tenement closes and homes during the daytime, as it did to skilled workers themselves.[12]

These 'respectable' workers cannot by any means be categorised as 'atypical' of their class. W. L. Guttsman, among others, has demonstrated how the Social Democratic working classes possessed cultural and ideological attitudes which stressed their desire to achieve recognition and integration within (bourgeois) society.[13] In the economic realm such attitudes included the acceptance, implicitly at least, on the part of some Social Democrats that the capitalist economic system would survive, develop, and even prosper for the foreseeable future. The task of trade unionists and socialists in these circumstances was to maximise benefits within the existing order, which could involve collaboration as much as confrontation. It is not as if the left of the Social Democratic movement had abandoned its Marxist principles, nor did sometimes bitter strikes cease to occur, but many in the labour movement became receptive to the argument that higher wages and living standards could be achieved through productivity gains. A more efficient economy might deliver benefits throughout society. This inherently collaborative notion could be reconciled relatively painlessly with the National Socialist concept of *Volksgemeinschaft* and was to become a significant factor in labour relations and wage fixing during the Third Reich – and indeed in the post-war Federal Republic. During Weimar, it must be said, such ideas found a foothold only in the Social Democratic (and Catholic) sections of the labour movement; the Communist minority reacted with undisguised fury to these notions of 'collaboration' with the class enemy (see Documents 58, 61).

Gunther Mai has shown how political attitudes within the Social Democratic movement could sometimes be very similar and it could, as previously noted, be argued that the Social Democratic leadership, which had in the wake of the war and the trauma of the peace settlement espoused the notion of national communal solidarity (*Volksgemeinschaft*) in its Görlitz Programme of 1921, made a fatal error when it returned to the concept of class struggle in the Heidelberg Programme of 1925[14] – partly in order to accommodate left-wing, Independent Socialists who had rejoined the party after the breakup of the USPD, partly at the prompting of trade union leaders. It had created ideological space for a National Socialist trade union movement by fatally underestimating the widespread desire among the working class for emancipation and justice within the existing society and by underestimating the extent and depth of working-class nationalist feeling.

William Brustein has advanced similar arguments regarding the NSDAP's membership and electorate, claiming that the National Socialists' commitment to social mobility and advancement appealed strongly to many workers – not least in the heavy staple industries where low levels of capital utilisation, lower wages and poor job prospects prevailed for much of the Weimar era. An autarkic economy with high levels of military expenditure, such as that advocated by the Nazis, offered a practical way out of the stagnation of the Weimar years.[15] It is significant that the National Socialist Factory Cells began to appear during the late 1920s without finance or encouragement from NSDAP headquarters – if anything the reverse was the case – and that the resulting NSBO grafted on many aspects of conventional trade union behaviour and practice to an ideology stressing workingclass interests within a national, German community where solidarity would count for a great deal more than individual liberties. An ideological and programmatic base for an element of workingclass participation in and identification with the National Socialist state had, evidently, been laid down (see Documents 55–57).

Whether any of this would have amounted to much in less

unstable times is a very moot question. However, the onset of the Great Depression and the failure, or at best the inability, of the Social Democratic movement to do more than stem the erosion of jobs, income and working-class political rights provided the National Socialist movement with its opportunity. The switch of former Social Democratic voters, the growth of the NSBO, the stream of workers into the NSDAP and the swelling ranks of the SA bore eloquent testimony to the Nazis' powers of mobilisation and integration at a time when much around them was disintegrating.

The Communist Party was an astute observer of this process and in its internal literature emphasised the profound sense of disillusionment and of lost opportunity which had gripped much of the working class at this time. The attitude of many working-class Nazis to the 1918–19 Revolution is important here for it is very much at variance with the commonplace view that Nazi supporters wished to reverse the effects of 1918–19 by radical means. Working-class Nazis frequently expressed the view that 1918 had been a wasted opportunity, that the SPD had botched the Revolution and that the signing of the Versailles Treaty had been the final straw. In other words the SPD was not criticised for moving too far, too fast, but for doing too little or the wrong thing (see Document 57). The KPD regarded this element of the NSDAP's constituency as moving leftwards (from the SPD) although insufficiently far left; the NSDAP acted for them as a halfway house between Social Democracy and Communism. Similarly the NSBO frequently criticised the official trade unions for their lack of willpower and their inability to defend working-class interests. Any notion of a 'Red' or Marxist menace was confined to the alleged propensity for Social Democratic or trade union functionaries to line their own pockets whilst neglecting the interests of their constituents. They were regarded as an integral part of the 'system' which had favoured sectional or individual interests and failed the wider national community demonstrably and spectacularly (see Document 56). In this respect too one can appreciate why the Communists regarded these particular Nazis as more to the left than the Social Democrats, although at the end of the day the Nazis' advocacy of an ethnic as against a class solidarity made any left-right distinctions largely irrelevant.

The National Socialists' relationship with the Communist Party (KPD) itself was altogether less straightforward. Voters switched from the KPD to the NSDAP during the early 1930s, but only in particularly large numbers in the March election of 1933. Some Communist Party members were former National Socialists and vice versa, but the numbers were small. There were transfers of members between the SA and the Communist Red Front – in both directions – but numerically significant switches appear to have been restricted to the autumn of 1932, when disillusioned SA members turned to the Communists, and early 1933 when Communists turned to the SA. A similar pattern is evident for the NSBO. In the spring of 1933 it attracted voting support and members from the Communist Revolutionary Trade Union Opposition (RGO), but large-scale movements are not evident before that. In essence it appears that each side attracted considerable numbers of supporters from the other at particularly critical times; either when one was apparently faced by terminal crisis (the NSDAP in late 1932) or when one had triumphed conclusively (the NSDAP in early 1933).

Both organisations seem to have sensed that one or the other would, eventually, take all. SA commanders, for example, repeatedly voiced concern that their men might desert to the KPD were the National Socialist movement to confront failure. Communist leaders were fearful that the National Socialists were poaching potential KPD recruits and were haunted by the possibility of the unemployed working classes switching to the Nazis (see Document 33). Eventually, during 1933, a very large proportion of the male unemployed working class did indeed join the SA.

It remains to be asked why the Nazis' mobilisation of a sizable working-class constituency remained largely unremarked during the early 1930s. It was, after all, well understood at the time that the NSDAP had triumphed in Protestant, lower middle-class circles. The pattern of the Nazi advance probably provides the most convincing explanation, for whilst entire middle-class organisations or identifiable milieux had been penetrated by, or had even switched to the National Socialists, the workers usually joined as individuals or sometimes as members of communities which lacked any pronounced class profile or awareness. The Social Democratic political and trade union organisations remained intact until forcibly suppressed by the National Socialist administration in early 1933, and even monarchist bodies which organised factory labour, such as the Stahlhelm, maintained their integrity until after the Nazi takeover. The switch of individual Social Democrats or trade unionists to the National Socialists occurred simultaneously with, and was partly obscured by, the debilitating effects of unemployment on membership levels and was further obscured by the aggressive, if relatively unsuccessful Communist assault on the Social Democratic movement. Exceptions, involving the switch of working-class milieux *en bloc* were relatively unusual although they did occur in certain areas, such as Baden's Black Forest region and in south-western Saxony (and parts of Thuringia) where, as Claus-Christian Szejnmann shows, a previously powerful socialist movement had atrophied.[16]

By 1932 the SPD began to suspect that the Nazis' advance was not confined to the middle classes, but self-interest and the party's Marxist convictions combined with the opacity of the evidence to stifle any thorough reappraisal of National Socialism. When the Nazis' volume of working-class support became all too evident during mid-1932 the SPD blamed non-Marxist workers, or even erstwhile Communists for the catastrophe (see Document 32). The KPD understood better what was happening, and their belief that individual workers, socialist and non-socialist alike, were switching to the Nazis in significant numbers has been vindicated by recent research. Of course it was in the Communists' interest to blame the SPD in particular for this catastrophe, but even the KPD stopped short of highlighting Nazi successes in their mass circulation literature. It is in internal party documents and party journals with a restricted circulation that the expression of its fears is found.

So what attracted working-class Germans to National Socialism? Clearly a range of factors was at work: the effects of the Depression on day-to-day life, aspects of working-class culture and politics in Weimar, and issues less immediately related to class. There seems little doubt that some working-class Nazis were aggressive exponents of their own class interests, but it could not have escaped their notice that the movement as a whole was not largely, still less exclusively working-class. Even their own NSBO cells, SA companies and, more especially, party branches were usually socially heterogeneous. The middle classes, particularly office and sales staff, were there in force. To generalise, therefore, working-class National Socialism might be viewed not as an expression of class solidarity, but as an attempt (however inchoate the ideals of individual members) to forge a new social solidarity which, being *völkisch*, would transcend class, but not nation. The national ethnic community was to serve as the new locus of identity and interest: a proposition not without its difficulties, but no less acceptable to workers than the Communists' advocacy of undiluted class warfare.

Notes

1 Martin Broszat, *The Hitler State. The foundation and development of the internal structure of the Third Reich*, trans. J. Hiden, London, New York, 1981, ch. 2.

2 Reichsorganisationsleiter der NSDAP (ed.), *Partei-Statistik. Stand 1. Januar 1935*, Munich, 1935.

3 Jürgen W. Falter, *Hitlers Wähler*, Munich, 1991, chs. 5–7, esp. pp. 110–17, 198–230.

4 Falter, *Wähler*, p. 116. The NSDAP won around 350,000 voters net from the KPD. The other 150,000 voters gained were offset by a switch of 150,000 Nazi voters to the KPD over the final Weimar elections.

5 Detlef Mühlberger, *Hitler's Followers. Studies in the Sociology of the Nazi Movement*, London, New York, 1991, chs. 2–7.

6 Jürgen W. Falter, 'Die Jungmitglieder der NSDAP zwischen 1925 und 1933. Ein demographisches und soziales Profil', in Wolfgang R. Krabbe (ed.), *Politische Jugend in der Weimarer Republik*, Dortmund, 1993, pp. 202–21. See esp. table 7.

7 William Brustein, 'Blue Collar Nazism: The German Working Class and the Nazi Party', in Conan Fischer (ed.), *Weimar, the Working Classes and the Rise of National Socialism*, Oxford, 1995, forthcoming.

8 Richard J. Hamilton, *Who Voted for Hitler?*, Princeton, 1982, p. 38 ff.

9 Mühlberger, *Hitler's Followers*, chs. 5 and 6.

10 Ingrid Buchloh, *Die nationalsozialistische Machtergreifung in Duisburg. Eine Fallstudie*, Duisburg, 1980, p. 123.

11 Falter, *Wähler*, p. 311, table 8.7.

12 Eve Rosenhaft, 'The Unemployed in the Neighbourhood: Social Dislocation and Political Mobilisation in Germany 1929–1933', in Richard Evans and Dick Geary (eds.), *The German Unemployed. Experiences and Consequences of Mass Unemployment from the Weimar Republic to the Third Reich*, London, Sydney, 1987, pp. 219–23.

13 W. L. Guttsman, *Workers' Culture in Weimar Germany. Between Tradition and Commitment*, New York, Oxford, Munich, 1990, pp. 44–53, 54–64.

14 Gunther Mai, 'National Socialist Factory Cell Organisation and German Labour Front . . .', in Fischer (ed.), *Weimar*.

15 Brustein, 'Blue Collar Nazism'.

16 Claus-Christian Szejnmann, 'The Rise of the Nazi Party in the Working-Class Milieu of Saxony', in Fischer (ed.), *Weimar*.

Conclusion

The rise of Nazism remains a hauntingly compelling episode, primarily because Hitler's seizure of power led on to the methodical slaughter of millions of innocent people. But as Juan J. Linz observes, '[fascist] movements and their appeal cannot be understood from the perspective of an analysis of fascist parties in power'.[1] Few would quarrel with this, yet the burden of hindsight cannot be cast off lightly and has often impelled historians to corral Weimar National Socialism away from the mainstream of German or European history and to belittle its capabilities and wider prospects. Its leaders can appear as freakish, marginal men, its policies irrational, its organisational methods unsustainable. There is some merit in such observations, but they have been overworked by historians who, to borrow John Plamenatz's words, seek 'assurance that man is moving in a definite and desirable direction', that the course of history is able to lend 'dignity and importance' to the individual.[2] Milan Hauner complained that non-German historians in particular have too often underestimated National Socialism,[3] but underestimation is a useful tool if Hitler and his movement are to be excluded from the twentieth-century mainstream. Zeev Sternhell notes that a reluctance to attribute a fundamental substance to fascism could be because 'in conceding fascism a theoretical dimension one might have granted it a place and a significance in the history of our times, which many people of the right and the left . . . were reluctant to do'.[4] Sternhell, however, does not regard Nazism as fascist, of which more later.

122

This understandable desire to confine National Socialism to a historical blind alley is possibly reinforced by widespread contemporary adherence to beliefs in secular progress which have their roots in the eighteenth-century Enlightenment. Such notions lend the concept of modernity an unmistakably moral dimension, making intermittent attempts to investigate the relationship between National Socialism and the modern contentious to say the least. Most of this work has focused on the Nazi state, but Detlev Peukert confronted the linkages between what he regarded as a rapid, disruptive and controversial process of modernisation in Weimar Germany and the rise of Nazism. The latter, he argued, combined traditional, 'restorationalist' values with aspects of modernity, including a 'new spirit of quasi-egalitarianism', dynamism, modern techniques of propaganda and notions of technocratic efficiency.[5] This echoes Sternhell's observations on the technocratic, modernising dimension of fascism, but his argument parts company from Peukert's in lending this dimension a socialist character: 'the result of a revision of Marxism and an expression of the attempt to adapt socialism to modern conditions on both the ideological and tactical planes'.[6] Central to Sternhell's case is the declining significance of the class struggle à la Marx in twentieth-century Europe and the growing importance of the nation and national solidarity, which would appear to constitute an essential dimension of Weimar Nazism. This line of reasoning lends fascism an unequivocal place in the mainstream of twentieth-century historical development; and in relegating orthodox socialism to the nineteenth century to take its place alongside classical capitalism, it turns liberal and socialist perceptions of fascism's historical locus on their heads.

However, it would be wrong to exploit Sternhell's analysis any further, for he rejects the possibility of discussing Nazism in this context at all because of its racialism: 'Nazism cannot, as I see it, be treated as a mere variant of fascism: its emphasis on biological determinism rules out all efforts to deal with it as such.'[7] This might arguably be less valid for Nazism during its Weimar phase when biological racialism was not promoted to any great extent, but the relationship between fascism and Nazism remains contentious none the less. Karl Dietrich Bracher concurs with Sternhell's assessment, arguing that the equation of fascism and

Nazism downgrades the horror of the latter[8] (although in present-day political language the term fascism has been very much tarred with the Nazi brush). Linz prevaricates a little in typifying National Socialism as 'a distinctive branch grafted on the fascist tree'.[9] Ian Kershaw, however, concludes that on balance the similarities between Nazism and 'other brands of fascism are profound, not peripheral',[10] arguing that the course and outcome of the First World War had comparable effects in particular on German and Italian political life and that in both countries fascism developed as a mass movement which challenged the existing order, but simultaneously provided the bourgeois classes with a riposte to and escape from the demands of organised socialism.

The waters of theoretical debate are muddied further by contested attempts to include National Socialism within a totalitarian model which includes the Marxist-Leninist system of rule, and by argument over the degree to which Hitler's contribution to Nazism made it unique. At one extreme of this discussion Hitler is viewed as a relatively insignificant individual who derived his substance largely from his role as titular leader of the Nazi movement. At the other, in complete contrast, National Socialism is regarded as 'Hitlerism' and thus the incorporation of his ideological and strategic objectives. The role of class interests in the rise of Nazism has produced a substantial body of theory which focuses on the role of the middle classes in the affair, but it is here in particular that recent empirical work has created difficulties which are only currently being addressed. Small wonder, then, that Eugen Weber concluded somewhat wearily: 'We know too much nowadays to explain very much. We certainly know too little to explain anything thoroughly.'[11]

This was not intended as an abdication of responsibility, nor should such sentiments serve to question the cumulative value of decades of research, discussion and debate. None the less, as a subject of historical enquiry Nazism continues to present a moving target, making the reassessment of erstwhile orthodoxies as necessary as the discovery and presentation of fresh evidence. During the past decade it has become increasingly clear that the Nazi movement was not a purely middle-class affair during the Weimar era, at least in terms of its constituency, but this discovery has elicited a variety of responses. Some historians have, as shown, continued to regard National Socialism as a middle-class *rassemblement* to which, however, a sizable number of non-socialist workers appended themselves. This line of argument does least violence to the traditional middle-class model of Nazism, for while it demands a reappraisal of the politics and ethos of certain working-class Germans, it need not necessarily question traditional perceptions of the relationship between the NSDAP and the (Protestant) middle classes. Much more radical is the suggestion that class-based analysis might not contribute greatly to our understanding of Nazism at all. Jane Caplan and Thomas Childers are among those who have emphasised the importance of the racialist and feminist dimensions, as well as the value of detailed insights provided by *Alltagsgeschichte* (the history of everyday life).[12] Michael Burleigh and Wolfgang Wippermann have proposed that National Socialism can, indeed, best be understood in terms of its racial objectives,[13] but these arguments have the greatest force when applied to the history of the Third Reich. It was then that the NSDAP's racialist policies became substance, with consequences that are well understood. Another approach, recognising that some 40 per cent of NSDAP members and voters were working-class (as well as a majority of SA and NSBO members), has seen the Nazi movement as a social coalition, a *Volksbewegung*, which accommodated the interests of bourgeois and workers alike by offering them a place in a national ethnic community, or *Volksgemeinschaft*. It is this line of interpretation that has been supported most strongly here.

Precisely what this *Volksgemeinschaft* meant to citizens of the Weimar Republic and how it might be placed in German history is less clear. Germans from a wide variety of social backgrounds supported the Nazis, but had distinctive reasons for doing so which often related to this same socio-economic diversity. As a corollary to this, their expectations of what a National Socialist administration might yield them also differed widely, which suggests that the complete abandonment of 'class analysis' in the study of Nazism would be unwarranted. However, the NSDAP was more than just a diffuse aggregation of particular interests; its *völkisch* ideology through which its programme acquired a degree of integrity demands closer examination and explanation.

A first and fairly obvious point is that the *Volksgemeinschaft* was essentially an inclusive, integrative concept whose perceived unreclaimable enemies within Germany itself could be numbered at less than a million. The NSDAP had trouble in persuading time-served Socialist and Catholic voters in particular that its *völkisch* programme was for them, but they were always a target group for Nazi policymakers and propagandists and, as we now know, they were not always immune as such to the appeal of National Socialism. The narrower focus and partisan nature of Weimar political life has become almost legendary and the Socialists and Communists had been sucked into this mode of politics to some extent by default. Firstly the SPD and KPD regarded each other with all the contempt and loathing of erstwhile partners after a messy and protracted divorce. And then they discovered that the goods and chattels of their former union were less extensive than their nineteenth-century ideological mentors had predicted. The fact that a diffuse working-class electorate constituted under half the enfranchised population posed immediate problems for any party whose programme and ideology was predicated primarily on working-class interests. In placing collective interests above sectional, national interests above class, the Nazis were simultaneously providing a diagnosis of Weimar's problems and prescribing a cure.

The place of nation and nationhood in the appeal of National Socialism is not straightforward. The *Volksgemeinschaft* was not originally a Nazi concept, for it found expression in some conservative, Catholic and Social Democratic circles before the First World War. The war itself and its traumatic aftermath lent *völkisch* ideology substance and far greater resonance, but only the NSDAP succeeded in promoting this ideology with sufficient consistency and conviction to exert a wide appeal. As the concept of *Volksgemeinschaft* became essentially Nazi it is perhaps understandable that the NSDAP's enemies came to regard it as representative of a definable set of interests; these other parties were themselves bound to sectional interests and usually judged Nazism by their own standards. Thus for the SPD and KPD, who viewed history in the last resort as the history of class struggle, it was logical to perceive Nazism as an incorporation of middle-class interests dressed up in fresh rhetoric. This view of Nazism was not confined to its left-wing political enemies, for numerous scholars of every political shading have since subscribed to comparable lines of analysis. Notable has been Ernst Nolte who, in a series of major works, has interpreted Nazism as a specifically bourgeois reaction to the spectre of Bolshevism.[14]

It is certainly true that millions of middle-class Germans sought deliverance by the Nazi movement from Marxism in any shape or form, but it now appears that they tended to perceive this salvation more as an escape from class and sectional politics altogether than as the pursuit of class politics by new and more radical means. It has always been accepted that National Socialist rhetoric pointed in this direction, but as long as it appeared that the Nazi movement was essentially a middle-class phenomenon, many historians quite understandably concluded that the concept of *Volksgemeinschaft* was imbued with a middle-class character. In short it was little more than a fig-leaf covering middle-class interests. However, the now unmistakable presence of millions of working-class Germans among the Nazi movement's activists and supporters lends much more substance to the NSDAP's original claims, not least because an identification with collective national interests evidently informed working-class Nazis as much as it did middle-class supporters. In this regard there was clearly a contrast between the conservative elites who sought to instrumentalise National Socialism for their own ends during the final crisis of the Depression years and the Nazis themselves. This is not to argue that Nazi supporters wished their identities and interests to be subsumed within a homogenous mass, and the NSDAP's plethora of ancillary formations testified to the care it took to subscribe to its supporters' particular interests and aspirations. However, the National Socialists constantly stressed that they would accommodate these diverse interests, accord them their rightful place within a harmonious *Volksgemeinschaft*; it was never proposed that a future Nazi state would be a workers' state, a peasants' state, a bourgeois state, or whatever.

In this particular sense the rise of Nazism relates to a wider pattern of twentieth-century European historical development which has witnessed an unmistakable, if hesitant, move away from social confrontation towards attempts at conciliation and integration within national political systems. During the inter-war period examples included Italian fascism or the Spanish Falange which exerted an appeal to corporatist-minded labour as well as to middle-class elements, but this process has generally owed much to the values of the Enlightenment and the subsequent revolutionary movements which placed great emphasis on the dignity and rights of the individual – in theory at least. Furthermore the concept of citizenship served to mediate between individuals and society's collective interests, added to which there has recently been an increasing willingness to recognise the interests of minority cultures and smaller historic nations subsumed within larger states. These notions, of course, were entirely alien to National Socialism, whose intolerant, predatory, *völkisch* vision of the national community had origins not in the Western Enlightenment but in the lands east of Weimar Germany from whence it infiltrated westwards. The specific circumstances surrounding the crises and death agonies of the Habsburg and Hohenzollern Empires and the subsequent moral and material crises of the Weimar Republic permitted the triumph of these *völkisch* prescriptions outwith their natural habitat, where they then mingled with older values of duty and a newer concept of technocratic efficiency to deadly effect.

This was neither a simple nor an inevitable process, for a great many variables combined to generate popular support for National Socialism. The translation of this popularity into power then owed much to the disastrous miscalculations of the German elites at the end of Weimar. Foremost among the variables was the figure of Hitler himself, without whom the development of Nazism as it existed would have been inconceivable. His ability to contribute to ideology, policy and propaganda, and to function as the organisational linchpin of a turbulent movement, his ability also to project charisma in the strict sense of the word, made him indispensable. Given his importance, it is fair to conclude that National Socialism in its classic form has been consigned to the graveyard of history along with its leader.

However, among the complex web of historical forces and influences which explain the rise (and subsequent conduct) of Nazism there are also mundane factors which belong to the typical experiences of modern capitalist societies. Liberals have often sought explanations for fascism and Nazism in the stresses unleashed by the switch from a pre-capitalist to a capitalist form of society, thus perceiving these ideologies as symptoms of a developmental crisis on the road to mature capitalism. Such developmental stresses clearly played a role in the affair, for the

Nazis often harked on traditional symbols and values in their propaganda and policies, but National Socialism also fed on pressures within capitalist society itself. These pressures could take the form of crises such as the Great Depression, but it should also be remembered that the upheavals which accompanied the rise of capitalism were not a once-and-for-all occurrence, to be followed by a period of retrenchment and stability. If anything the pace of socio-economic change, already disorienting during the initial process of industrialisation and urbanisation, has continued to accelerate to breakneck speed, and changes to accepted patterns of morality, the shaky legitimacy of some governmental systems, the presence of structural as well as cyclical unemployment, and periodic demands for or the actual emergence of 'strong leaders' remain the common currency of the contemporary European experience.

These features, of course, were common also to the origins of National Socialism and fascism, and at critical moments commentators can still ask anxiously: 'Is Britain, Spain, Russia . . . Weimar?', with all the obvious connotations therein. Given the absence of Hitler and the weakness of anti-Semitic *völkisch* ideology in contemporary Western and Central Europe (lurid press reports notwithstanding), these fears are probably overstated. However, it is unquestionable that the present liberal economic and social order within the European Union is simply an episode on the path of historical development. The railway tracks run on beyond the horizon and we are no more at history's destination than, say, was Hegel's Prussia.

Whether something comparable to Nazism will at some point inherit the European body politic is another matter. The moral traumas bequeathed by Nazism have left an indelible stain on the German and European present, left many Germans haunted by and alienated from their own past, and have greatly complicated the task of understanding why and how Hitler's movement came to power. To focus on the mundane would be grossly inadequate, to focus exclusively on the lurid distorts. Karl Marx openly voiced scepticism about the capacity of history to repeat itself and historians who make detailed predictions about the future find that they are at their most consistent in being wrong. There is sufficient evidence to justify the hope that National Socialism was indeed a particular response to events at a particular time in a particular place; future European upheavals will assume (or may already be assuming) their own distinctive form.

Notes

1   Juan J. Linz, 'Some Notes Toward a Comparative Study of Fascism in Historical Perspective', in Walter Laqueur (ed.), *Fascism: A Reader's Guide. Analyses, Interpretations, Bibliography*, Harmondsworth, 1979, p. 22.

2   John Plamenatz, *Man and Society. Political and Social Theories from Machiavelli to Marx*, 2nd edn., London and New York, 1992, vol. 3, p. 326.

3   Milan Hauner, 'Did Hitler Want a World Dominion', *Journal of Contemporary History*, 13, 1978, p. 16.

4   Zeev Sternhell, 'Fascist Ideology', in Laqueur (ed.), *Fascism*, pp. 326–7.

5   Detlev Peukert, *The Weimar Republic: the crisis of classical modernity*, trans. Richard Deveson, London, 1991, p. 236 ff.

6   Sternhell, *Ideology*, p. 372.

7   *Ibid.*, p. 328.

8   Karl Dietrich Bracher, 'The Role of Hitler: Perspectives of Interpretation', in Laqueur (ed.), *Fascism*, p. 202.

9   Linz, 'Notes', p. 24.

10   Ian Kershaw, *The Nazi Dictatorship. Problems and Perspectives of Interpretation*, London, 1985, p. 40.

11   Eugen Weber, 'Revolution? Counter–revolution? What Revolution?', in Laqueur (ed.), *Fascism*, p. 524.

12   Thomas Childers and Jane Caplan (eds.), *Reevaluating the Third Reich*, New York, London, 1993, pp. 3–4.

13   Michael Burleigh and Wolfgang Wippermann, *The Racial State. Germany 1933–1945*, Cambridge, 1991.

14   Ernst Nolte, *The Three Faces of Fascism*, London, 1965; *Der Europäische Bürgerkrieg: Nationalsozialismus und Bolschewismus*, Berlin, 1987.

Selected documents

National Socialism and the Weimar establishment

The key institutions in Weimar Germany adopted strikingly different stances when it came to dealing with the Nazis. Most of the State governments and police forces did their best to contain and even suppress the Nazi movement. The same could not always be said for the central government, the army or the conservative elites whose indulgence of Nazism was not always repaid or even appreciated by Hitler's movement.

Document 1
The Hessian authorities deplore SA violence

In April 1930 the national and State security chiefs held a conference in Berlin during which the burgeoning National Socialist movement was discussed at length. A Prussian ban on the SA had resulted in storm-troopers from the Prussian city of Frankfurt-am-Main raiding neighbouring Hessen.
From: Bundesarchiv R134/58 (207).

> If a sufficient police presence is not maintained the National Socialists do not balk at acts of terrorism. In this regard, of course, non-Hessian supporters are most prominent. The Frankfurt SA is disagreeably prominent in such activities; its membership includes especially vicious villains who belonged to the Communist Red Front before it was banned.

Document 2
The army trains the SA

While the State police forces struggled to contain SA violence during 1931, army chiefs moved to provide it with training. They opposed SA leaders' ambitions ultimately to displace the army, but were relatively enthusiastic about the SA's potential as a paramilitary counterweight to the republican and revolutionary left and a potential source of manpower, eventually, for the army itself. The first training courses were held in the Ruhr District and its surrounding area. Here the Central German SA, based in Dresden, reports to headquarters.

From: Bayerisches Hauptstaatsarchiv München, So I 1533, Der Gruppenführer Mitte. An den Obersten SA-Führer. Dresden, 29.6.1931.

With reference to the communication of 25 June I report that thus far the army has made contact with the SA in Leipzig and Döbeln. In Leipzig, so far, this has only involved students, in Döbeln individual SA members have been offered training.

On the basis of the information received by Munich [SA Headquarters], the Group has verbally informed SA officers that they can comply with army requests of this type and that we ourselves find it thoroughly desirable that the SA is afforded an opportunity for physical training.

Document 3
The fragile Harzburg front

In October 1931 the DNVP, Stahlhelm and National Socialists held a spectacular joint rally in the spa town of Bad Harzburg. It was intended to seal an alliance between the elements of the nationalist right, but as the newspaper the *Bayrischer Kurier* reported, Hitler was uncooperative even at the meeting itself. The scene was set for future relations. The traditional right came increasingly to see good relations with Hitler as indispensable; he exploited their goodwill with ill-disguised contempt.

From: 'SA gegen Stahlhelm', *Bayrischer Kurier*, No. 287, 14 October 1931.

Whilst Hugenberg's newspapers printed bombastic reports on the Harzburg Rally and its 'splendid' execution, it looked considerably different behind the scenes. A massive fraternal dispute flared up between Hitler and Seldte [leader of the Stahlhelm]. For after the military religious service, during the march-off from the parade ground, a row broke out between the Stahlhelm and the National Socialists. The Stahlhelm demanded that it march off first. But the National Socialists simply left, marched past Hitler and the Stahlhelm leaders, and, as the last National Socialist went by, Adolf Hitler fell in behind his SA men. Outrage within the Stahlhelm over this, Hitler was no longer to be allowed to attend the banquet, and only shortly before the start of the big event was the conflict set aside after discussions between Hitler and Hugenberg. But the rivalry between the National Socialists, the German Nationalists and the Stahlhelm became more and more apparent during the subsequent course of the rally. How on earth will things turn out if the 'Front' has actually to take power?

Document 4
Bavaria fears Nazi anarchy

Relations between the National Socialists and the political right deteriorated during the autumn of 1932. Hitler still insisted on absolute power, but his movement was faced with an imminent electoral setback. Conservative Bavaria feared for its safety.

From: 'Und die SA?', *Regensburger Anzeiger*, 270, 30 September 1932, p. 2.

Not only will 6 November fail to deliver the goods, it will result in a net loss of seats, whether this is thirty or fifty being irrelevant. Its glorious advance will be crushed . . . and millions will be robbed of their hopes for a Third Reich. We must prepare for this. There are almost a million vagrants loose on the highways of Germany, alienated from work.

. . . Empty-handed, despairing in the SA Command's policies, faith in the Third Reich lost, homeless and penniless elements will, like the peasants of the Thirty Years' War, roam the countryside. The impoverished villages and farms can no more help these people than can the remote central authorities. Has the authoritarian Reich government taken precautions? There is one which Bavaria, patriotic and with its picturesque villages can take: the strengthening of the Bavarian Guard to a degree at which it can prevent robbery and arson. For behind the despairing SA men grins the MASK OF MOSCOW!

Document 5
The DNVP holds on to its votes

The DNVP's last stronghold was in the rural north-east of Germany. Here, on the great landed estates, the National Socialists were up against vote rigging and the dragooning of farm workers into the Stahlhelm, as a Nazi report drafted in March 1933 makes clear.

From: Staatliches Archivlager Göttingen, Rep 240 C43a. Kreis Darkehmen, 15 March 1933.

> DNVP. Its strength lies in the Stahlhelm and the Landowners' Association. In the District elections they not only managed to hold on to their vote, but actually to increase it. The reason for this is that the District administration has so far been in honest hands, in which the DNVP has been decisive. A notable feature of the District election results was that the labour force on various estates with German Nationalist owners voted almost solidly for the DNVP. A certain degree of interference occurred in many cases, as was to be expected.
>
> The Stahlhelm possesses a strong organisation here (strength 1,200). It is overwhelmingly pro-German Nationalist.

The ideology and ethos of Nazism

German National Socialism lacked any great guiding philosopher, remained bereft of any major seminal works (*pace Mein Kampf!*), and yet in its *völkisch* critique of contemporary German society developed a consistency and sense of conviction which was repeated again, and again, in speeches and writings to considerable effect. Ultimately the vision of social reconciliation posited on the solidarity of the ethnic German people proved very persuasive.

Document 6
The young Hitler on Habsburg Vienna

In the multinational Habsburg Empire many Germans felt that their traditional political predominance was under threat in the early twentieth century. Adolf Hitler's insecurity, racialism and anti-Semitism – as described here by his youthhood friend August Kubizek – were typical of the time and place.

From: August Kubizek, *Young Hitler. The Story of our Friendship*, trans. E. V. Anderson, Maidstone, 1973, pp. 185–6.

When home-going workers passed us by, Adolf would grip my arm and say, 'Did you hear, Gustl? Czechs!'. Another time, we encountered some brickmakers speaking loudly in Italian, with florid gestures. 'There you have your German Vienna', he cried, indignantly.

This, too, was one of his oft-repeated phrases: 'German Vienna', but Adolf pronounced it with a bitter undertone. Was this Vienna, into which streamed from all sides, Czechs, Magyars, Croats, Poles, Italians, Slovaks, Ruthenians, and above all Galician Jews, still indeed a German city? In the state of affairs in Vienna my friend saw a symbol of the struggle of the Germans in the Hapsburg [*sic*] Empire. He hated the babel in the streets of Vienna, this 'incest incarnate' as he called it later. He hated this State, which ruined Germanism, and the pillars that supported this State: the reigning house, the Church, the nobility, the capitalists and the Jews. . . . His accumulated hatred of all forces which threatened the Germans was mainly concentrated upon the Jews, who played a leading role in Vienna.

Document 7
Dietrich Eckart writes on the Jewish question

Eckart argued that the Jews' alleged worldly ambition and materialism made their presence indispensable 'until the fulfilment of [mankind's] earthly mission', but he continued that this presence was essentially a necessary evil, for the Jews' values were, he claimed, nihilistic.

From: D. Eckart, 'Jewishness in and around Us: Fundamental Reflections', *Auf Gut Deutsch*, Jan.–Apr. 1919, in Barbara Miller Lane and Leila J. Rupp (eds.), *Nazi Ideology before 1933. A Documentaion*, Manchester, 1978 pp. 25–6.

Some time ago the Jew Martin Buber gave a lecture in Munich in which he vividly dealt with the future state in Palestine. Very vividly. The most important of his statements was the following hint, expressed unintentionally but with great sullenness: if this state should be founded and there should creep into it even the slightest trace of a supernatural tendency, then it would also have to be destroyed!

The secret of Jewishness could not have been revealed more

135

plainly. It wants the despiritualisation of the world and nothing else; but this would be the same as its annihilation.

While the Jews still live among us, everything they do comes to this, and must come to this. Their goal is the despiritualisation of mankind. Therefore they attempt to destroy every form behind which the living soul operates; because, as archmaterialists, they are of the insane opinion that the spiritual – only vaguely suspected by them – is connected as a matter of life and death with the form, and must be destroyed together with it. Therefore they are all without exception anarchists, consciously or unconsciously; indeed they cannot be anything but opponents of law and order, because these two bear in incomparable fashion the shining stamp of a purer world. Schiller calls order the daughter of heaven, and in Schiller, but especially in Goethe, there are innumerable proofs of the divine origin of law.

But no idea of state can be realised without law and order; they are the indispensable basis for it. Therefore the Jew, their deadly enemy, can never create a viable state in Palestine. Instead, the Chaos would come again, for this word means, correctly translated: the infinite emptiness; in German, nothingness.

Document 8
Eckart denounces capitalism and socialism as Jewish

In the following tract, published during the Bavarian Soviet rising in April 1919, Eckart argued that socialism and Bolshevism were essentially Jewish-inspired and led, but so was capitalism. Ethnic Germans had to reject both in order to reclaim the wealth created by their own hard labour.
From: Dietrich Eckart, 'To All Working People!', in Barbara Miller Lane and Leila J. Rupp (eds.), *Nazi Ideology before 1933. A Documentation*, Manchester, 1978, pp. 31–2.

Loan capital brings in money without work, brings it in through interest. I repeat: without lifting a finger the capitalist increases his wealth by lending this money. It grows by itself. No matter how lazy one is, if one has money and lends it out at interest, one can live high, and one's children don't need to work either, or one's grandchildren, or one's great-grandchildren, and so on to eternity! How unjust this is, how shameless – doesn't everyone feel it?

To infinity it grows, this loan capital, through compound interest. Just one example: In 1806 the house of Rothschild began its lending business with the millions entrusted to it by the abdicating elector of Hesse. Something over 10 million it would have been, certainly not more than twenty. Today, after 110 years, the wealth of the Rothschilds amounts to 40 billion!

THE HOUSE OF ROTHSCHILD OWNS FORTY BILLION!

Not million, but billion! If it continues in the same way, they will own 80 billion in 1935, 160 billion in 1950 and 320 billion in 1965. It sounds like the ravings of a madman, but it is true! The Rothschilds only need to administer their wealth, to see that it is nicely placed, they do not need to work, at least not what we understand by work.

But who provides them and their like with such an enormous amount of money? Interest has to come from somewhere after all, somewhere these billions and more billions have to be produced by hard labour! Who does this? You do it, nobody but you! That's right, it is your money, hard earned through care and sorrow, which is as if magnetically drawn into the coffers of these insatiable people.

. . . But we hear nothing of that, not a word! We hear again and again about the farmers, about heavy industry, about industry in general. And with a deafening cry, our leading revolutionaries restrict their nationalisation plans to these branches of the economy! 'There's nothing else there to socialise!' This is what they din into your ears every day until you believe it yourselves and are happy that their magnanimity cares about you so much. Smartly said and smartly done I admit. Do you know the amount of the capital of our entire industry?

THE INDUSTRIAL CAPITAL OF ALL OF GERMAN INDUSTRY AMOUNTS TO LESS THAN 12 BILLION!

. . . We are intentionally diverted to the far lesser evil so that we will not see the greatest evil, all-consuming loan capital. And this is the way it's been done from Marx and Lassalle up to Levien, Landauer and Mühsam. Haven't you opened your eyes yet?

Document 9
Joseph Goebbels on National Socialism

Writing in the mid-1920s, while associated with the Strasser brothers, Goebbels emphasised that National Socialism represented a fundamental break with the politics both of the bourgeoisie and of Marxism.

From: Joseph Goebbels, 'The Radicalising of Socialism', in Barbara Miller Lane and Leila J. Rupp (eds.), *Nazi Ideology before 1933. A Documentation*, Manchester, 1978, pp. 79–80.

There are people in our camp, not the worst ones, who learned something after 1918 and are therefore still learning after 1923. Today they see not only the falsification of the socialist idea in Marxism, but also, just as clearly and plainly, the falsification of nationalism in the so-called national parties and organisations of every hue. They are prepared to draw from these insights the necessary political conclusions. They turn just as sharply against middle-class views as against Marxist proletarian ones . . . For them the middle class, in its political organisations, has lost the right to take a stand against any consequence of the politics of this system just as much as has Marxism, because both are guilty of this system, because both have participated in this system and will continue to do so, whenever and wherever the stampede to the fodder trough permits it. Down with the madness of Marxism, for it is falsified socialism! Down with the madness of the so-called national opposition in the parties of the right! For it is falsified nationalism. These are the slogans which make socialism into nationalism and nationalism into socialism. For us any nationalist demand requires a socialist one; any radicalisation of the national will for freedom, a radicalisation of socialism. You consistently confuse system and person. But it is always the system itself which is in question, never its temporary supporters.

Document 10
Hitler on the wedding of nationalism and socialism

Hitler spoke in comparable terms at an election meeting in Karlsruhe in March 1928.

From Adolf Hitler, 'Tageskampf oder Schicksalskampf?', in B. Dusik (ed.), *Hitler. Reden Schriften Anordnungen. Februar 1925 bis Januar 1933*, vol. 2(2), Munich, 1992, Doc. 238. p. 737.

We can conclude that bourgeois nationalism has failed, and that the concept of Marxist socialism has made life impossible in the long run. These old lines of confrontation must be eradicated along with the old parties, because they are barring the nation's path into the future. We are eradicating them by releasing the two concepts of nationalism and socialism and harnessing them for a new goal, towards which we are working full of hope, for the highest form of socialism is burning devotion to the nation.

Document 11
Hitler advocates Social Darwinism

Like many contemporaries and predecessors, Hitler regarded history as the history of struggle. For him the struggle was between races, rather than between classes, as he made clear at an election meeting in Ingolstadt in March 1928.
Adolf Hitler, 'Um das Schicksal der Nation', in B. Dusik (ed.), *Hitler. Reden Schriften Anordnungen. Februar 1925 bis Januar 1933*, vol. 2(2), Munich, 1992, Doc. 245.

> The main motivating forces of life are self-preservation and the safeguarding of future generations, and politics is none other than the struggle of peoples for their existence. This urge to live is universal and governs the whole nation. The urge to live must lead to conflict because it is insatiable, while the basis of life, territory, is limited. Thus brutality rather than humanity is the basis of life! Man has become master of the world through conflict and continual struggle. It is not humanity, but rather rights based on strength and the pre-eminence of power which have prevailed. But mankind is not a uniform and equal mass. There are differences between races. The Earth has received its culture from elite peoples; what we see today is ultimately the result of the activity and the achievements of the Aryans. Decisive within each race, however, are the personalities it is able to produce. Personalities have created the cultural shape of mankind and not democratic majorities.

Document 12
Hitler on the economy and trade

Hitler's views on international trade possessed Social Darwinistic and, perhaps, Malthusian overtones. He would never have proposed a policy of 'export or die', arguing that Europe's dependence on international trade amounted to 'export then die'.
From: G. L. Weinberg (ed.), *Hitlers Zweites Buch. Ein Dokument aus dem Jahr 1928*, Stuttgart, 1961, p. 60.

> The international market is not unlimited. The number of industrialised nations has steadily increased. Almost all European nations suffer from an inadequate and unsatisfactory relationship between the size of their territory and their population and are consequently driven to export goods on the world market.

Recently the United States and, in the East, Japan, have been added to their number. This in itself has triggered a struggle for limited markets which will become commensurately tougher as the number of industrialised nations increases and, as a corollary, the available markets become more restricted. For whilst on the one hand, the number of nations fighting for a share of the world market increases, the market itself gradually shrinks, partly as a result of indigenous industrialisation, partly through a network of subsidiary enterprises which are increasingly established in such countries purely to serve capitalist interests.

Document 13
Hitler on war

With natural resources and land in limited supply, Hitler believed that it was the duty of a responsible government to organise society for war thoroughly, and as a matter of course.
From: G. L. Weinberg (ed.), *Hitlers Zweites Buch. Ein Dokument aus dem Jahr 1928*, Stuttgart, 1961, p. 69.

The task which therefore falls to all really great legislators and statesmen is not so much to prepare for war in a narrow sense, but rather to educate and train thoroughly a people so that to all reasonable intents and purposes its future appears inherently assured. In this way even wars lose their character as isolated, more or less violent surprises, instead becoming part of a natural, indeed self-evident pattern of thorough, well-secured, sustained national development.

Document 14
Hitler on nationalism and socialism

Here Hitler expounds his vision of an ethnically predicated socialism which was simultaneously nationalist.
From: G. L. Weinberg (ed.), *Hitlers Zweites Buch. Ein Dokument aus dem Jahr 1928*, Stuttgart, 1961, p. 78.

I am a German nationalist. That is to say I am true to my nation. All my thoughts and actions are dedicated to it. I am a socialist. I recognise no class or status group, but rather a community of people, tied by blood, united by language, subject to a comprehensive, uniform fate. I love the nation and hate only its present ruling majority parties, because I regard them every bit as unrepresentative of the greatness of my nation as they are of its welfare.

Document 15
Hitler on the elimination of class conflict

On 31 August 1930, at an election meeting in Kiel, Hitler claimed that the NSDAP stood above class conflict and would eliminate it in Germany.
From: Bundesarchiv Koblenz, NS26/57. Kundgebung in Kiel, 31.8.1930.

The NSDAP is an organisation which does not recognise proletarians, does not recognise bourgeois, farmers, manual workers and so on; instead it is an organisation based in all regions of Germany, composed of all social groups. If you ask one of us; 'Young man, what are you? Bourgeois? Proletarian?', he will smile; 'I am a German! I fight in my brown shirt.' That is indicative of our significance; we do not aspire to be anything else, we are all fighting for the future of a people. We are all equal in our ranks.

Document 16
Nazism and women's rights

The Nazis planned to rescind many rights which women had acquired through successive legal reforms and the Weimar constitution. Here a Social Democrat warns in a speech of the likely consequences for women of a Nazi victory. Paragraph 218 was the section of the Weimar constitution banning abortions. 'Racial treason' was defined by the Nazis as sexual intercourse between so-called Aryans and non-Aryans.
From: Bundesarchiv R134/70 (147-48) 2nd National Congress of Working Women, Berlin, 29 November 1930.

And there is another party which calls itself a workers' party that we need to expose; the National Socialist Workers' Party . . .
The Nazis are a reactionary party. They want doubly to uphold the repression of women and the denial of their rights. They object to women working in the factories, saying that women, after all, merely work to buy silk stockings and chocolates. They want to force women to bear children which they cannot afford to feed. For transgression of Paragraph 218 they demand imprisonment, for extreme cases of racial treason even the death penalty.

Selected documents

Document 17
Röhm evokes the concept of the front-line community

Ernst Röhm commanded the NSDAP's storm-troopers in 1924–25 and from 1931 until his death on Hitler's orders in mid-1934. As a veteran of the First World War, who had exhibited conspicuous bravery under fire, this former army captain loathed civilian society and was deeply contemptuous of the Weimar Republic. Here, on the tenth anniversary of Hitler's Munich *Putsch*, he voices this antipathy and sets out his ideological vision of the newly established Third Reich.
From: E. Röhm, 'Die Zehnjahresfeier der nationalsozialistischen Bluttaufe', *Der SA-Mann*, 2(45), p. 4.

When the civilians filched the leadership of our nation in November 1918, there was a great danger that our Fatherland would be plunged into bloody Bolshevik chaos, thanks to the incompetence of these so-called men of government. Their helplessness and cowardice drove them yet again to appeal to soldiers to save them or, as the soldiers saw it, yet again to save Germany . . .

Now the whole of Germany is infused once more with a genuine, positive, soldierly ethos. We soldiers understand this ethos, which constitutes the contemporary National Socialist political soldier's mission, to be: the community of all social ranks and classes, the fellowship of all who share the same language and blood, solidarity on days good and bad, the comradeship of all people good and true to the death.

Document 18
An SA sergeant expounds his version of Nazi ideology

The NSDAP's vision of the *Volksgemeinschaft* found resonance throughout the Nazi movement. Here an NCO in the storm-troopers sets out in 1933 his confused, sometimes disturbing version of the movement's ethos.
From: Hessisches Hauptstaatsarchiv Wiesbaden, 483/2190, 81st SA Regiment, Frankfurt-am-Main.

When National Socialism appeared it encountered political parties which were not founded on the inner man, his spiritual character and his ethos, but instead on something external – economic principles. The soul of the nation, however, remained entirely untouched by this, as was manifested unequivocally for the first time on 1 August 1914. Neither the economy, nor groups, nor particular organisations were decisive, but rather the soul of the nation. National Socialism developed of necessity from the latter. Our opponents therefore committed a fundamental error when equating us as a party with the Economic Party (*Wirtschaftspartei*), the Democrats or the Marxist parties. All these parties were only interest groups, they lacked soul, spiritual ties. Adolf Hitler emerged as bearer of a new political religion. This religion was born out of the German national awakening of 1 August 1914 and our people's great struggle between 1914 and 1918.

If we wish to comprehend the situation then we have to understand that on 1 August 1914 there were two types of people in Germany: the socially free and the socially repressed. The former were people with property, who were tied to the Fatherland through the ownership of land or property. The latter had no possessions, some had no dwelling, they certainly lacked any substance in their lives and were without faith. However, in the emergency of 1 August 1914 all German men were needed and thus even this second group, who couldn't really expect anything from this Fatherland, went enthusiastically to battle for this self-same Fatherland. That was the essential experience of the Great War and, in a manner of speaking, the miracle of German national unity which had occurred for the first time. This experience, however, entailed the obligation that all Germans within the Fatherland should no longer, as before, be bound together by words and charity, but by basic rights.

The German worker had always sought these rights, but in his search for social justice had fallen into the hands of a doctrine which did not grasp his inner being and soul, did not offer him a universal philosophy of life, but at best merely an economic principle . . .

We distinguish ourselves from the best nationalists of the old school, even in our conception of nationalism, through our readiness for sacrifice. The patriots' nationalism was usually merely the cloak under which economic advantage was disguised. Our nationalism is born of the necessity to achieve socialism within our borders. Whosoever is of our blood, whosoever is bound to us through soil and history and speaks our language is our ethnic comrade and has the right to be treated equally and be accorded equal rights. The Marxists were convinced that the class contradictions within the nation could only be eliminated through the proletarian world revolution, and since discontent prevailed in Germany, agitators surfaced here whose demagogic methods eventually became an end in themselves. As, however, the Fatherland stood up and cared for every ethnic comrade, Marxism was superfluous and eliminated. We insist on the nationalism of the national soul, something which, for example, the Stahlhelm has not yet understood; it perceives nationalism as the state's military-political duties. Hitler's nationalism is bound to socialism, for we can only be strong externally if we are just and therefore united internally. Our socialism is justice. . . .

Policy

The National Socialists produced a wide range of policy statements between 1920 and 1933, some of a general programmatic nature, others addressing the concerns of particular constituences, such as agriculture or labour. The *völkisch* dimension of Nazi ideology ran through these statements as a unifying strand.

Document 19
The NSDAP's Programme, the Twenty-Five Points

Drafted by a number of leading Nazis, including Hitler, in early 1920, the NSDAP's Programme, or Twenty-Five Points, was short on detail but carved out a distinctive niche for the new party. Too collectivist to be liberal, too emancipatory to be conservative, too nationalist and populist to be orthodox socialist, and openly racialist, the Programme was lent a certain coherence by its *völkisch* ideological foundations. This generally accepted version was first published in 1923.

The Programme of the German Workers' Party is addressed to its era. Once the goals announced in it have been achieved, the leaders have no intention of setting new ones in order artificially to increase the discontent of the masses, merely thereby to permit the continuance of the party.

1. We demand the union of all Germans in a Greater Germany, on the basis of the right of self-determination of nations.

2. We demand equal rights for the German people in its dealings with other nations and the abrogation of the peace treaties of Versailles and St Germain.

3. We demand land and soil (colonies) for the nourishment of our people and the settlement of our surplus population.

4. Only he who is an ethnic comrade may be a citizen. Only he who is of German blood, regardless of religious denomination, can be an ethnic comrade. No Jew, therefore, can be an ethnic comrade.

5. Anyone who is not a citizen shall live in Germany only as a guest and must be regarded as being subject to the laws governing the conduct of aliens.

6. The right to make decisions in the realms of governance and legislation belongs uniquely to citizens.

We therefore demand that every public office, of whatever kind, whether national, state or local, be filled only by citizens.

We oppose the corrupting parliamentary system of filling posts merely according to party interests and without regard for character or ability.

7. We demand that the state pledge itself to assure the productivity and livelihood of its citizens above all others. If it is not possible to support the entire population, aliens (non-citizens) are to be expelled from the country.

8. Any further immigration of non-Germans is to be prevented. We demand that all non-Aryans who have entered Germany since 2 August 1914 shall be required forthwith to leave the Reich.

9. All citizens are to possess equal rights and duties.

10. It must be the foremost duty of every citizen to work mentally or physically. The activities of the individual may not conflict with the interests of the general public, but must be pursued within the framework of the community and for the good of all.

WE THEREFORE DEMAND:

11. Abolition of income not earned by labour or effort.

BREAKING THE BONDAGE OF INTEREST.

12. In view of the enormous sacrifice of blood and property which each and every war demands of a nation, personal enrichment as a result of war must be regarded as a crime against the nation. We therefore demand the outright confiscation of all war profits.

13. We demand nationalisation of all hitherto listed companies (trusts).

14. We demand that profits from the wholesale trade be redistributed.

15. We demand a generous expansion in provision for old age.

16. We demand the creation and maintenance of a healthy middle class; immediate communalisation of wholesale business premises and their leasing to small traders at low rents; that the most preferential consideration be shown to small businessmen in all public purchasing and contracting, whether national, state, or

local.

17. We demand land reform suited to our national requirements, enactment of a law for expropriation without compensation of land for communal purposes, abolition of interest on loans secured on land and the prevention of all speculation in land.

18. We demand ruthless prosecution of those whose activities are harmful to the common good. Sordid traitors, userers, profiteers and the like are to be punished with death, regardless of religious confession or race.

19. We demand that Roman Law, which serves the materialist world order, be replaced by German Common Law.

20. In order to allow every able and industrious German access to higher education and thus to achieve professional advancement, the state must undertake a thorough overhaul of our national educational system. The curriculum of every educational establishment must be adapted to the demands of practical life. The school must impart an understanding of state and public affairs at the earliest stage in the child's intellectual development. We demand the furtherance of gifted children from poor families at the state's expense, regardless of the the parents' status or profession.

21. The state must improve public health by protecting mothers and infants, prohibiting child labour, improving physical fitness through a statutory programme of gymnastics and sports, and by extensive support for clubs concerned with the physical training of youth.

22. We demand the abolition of a professional army and the formation of a national popular army.

23. We demand legal action against deliberate political falsehood and its dissemination through the press. In order to facilitate the creation of a German national press, we demand that:

a) all editors and contributors to German-language newspapers be ethnic comrades.

b) express permission from the state be required for non-German newspapers to appear. These are not to be printed in the German language.

c) non-Germans be prohibited by law from participating financially in or influencing German newspapers and that contravention thereof be punished by closure of the publishing house and immediate expulsion of non-Germans involved.

Newspapers not conducive to the national welfare are to be forbidden. We demand legal measures against any tendency in art and literature of a kind likely to undermine national life and the suppression of any institutions which militate against these demands.

24. We demand freedom for all religious denominations within the state as long they do not endanger it and do not violate the ethical and moral feelings of the German race.

The party, as such, subscribes to a positive Christianity without binding itself to a particular denomination. It opposes the Jewish materialistic spirit within and about us and is convinced that a lasting recovery of our nation can only be achieved from within on the principle:

THE COMMON INTEREST BEFORE INDIVIDUAL INTEREST

25. In order to realise the above we demand the creation of a strong central authority in Germany. The central Parliament must have unquestioned authority over the whole country and its entire organisation; and there must be Chambers based on corporate groups and occupation to execute within the federal states the general laws enacted by the Reich.

The leaders of the party swear that they will unswervingly seek fulfilment of the foregoing points, if necessary sacrificing their lives.

Document 20
Hitler on agricultural policy

The NSDAP made a determined effort to woo the farming population during the final years of Weimar. Here, in a party statement signed by Hitler in March 1930, but possibly penned by the Strassers, it is emphasised that the peasantry would find their place within a broadly based Nazi movement. The National Socialists saw little merit in special interest parties, such as the farmers' leagues, instead advocating the 'liberation' of the entire ethnic German people. In 1932 the leagues' electoral supporters, frustrated by their impotence, turned in large numbers to the Nazis.

Extracted from Barbara Miller Lane and Leila J. Rupp, *Nazi Ideology before 1933. A Documentation*, Manchester, 1978, pp. 122–3.

V. CORPORATE OCCUPATIONAL ORGANISATIONS ARE NOT ENOUGH; THE PEASANTRY CAN FIND DECISIVE AID ONLY FROM THE POLITICAL GERMAN LIBERATION MOVEMENT OF THE NSDAP.

The present distress of the farmers is part of the distress of the entire German people.

It is madness to believe that a single occupational group can exclude itself from the German community which shares in the same fate; it is a crime to set farmers and city dwellers against one another, for they are bound together for better or for worse.

Economic makeshift measures within the framework of the present political system cannot bring sweeping improvement; for the distress of the German people is rooted in its political enslavement, from which only political means can deliver it.

The old ruling political parties which led our people into slavery cannot be the leaders on the road to emancipation.

Corporate organisations will have important economic tasks in our future state, and can in this sense already carry on important preparatory work. But for the political war of liberation which must first create the prerequisites for a new economic order, they are unsuited. For this war cannot be carried on from the standpoint of a single occupational group; it must rather be carried on from the standpoint of the entire people.

The war of liberation against our oppressors and their taskmasters can be successfully led only by a political liberation movement which, although it fully recognises the significance of the farmers and of agriculture for the German workers as a whole, draws together the consciously German members of every occupation and rank.

This political liberation movement of the German people is the National Socialist German Workers' Party.

Document 21
Walther Darré on agricultural policy

Darré, as leader of the Agricultural Affairs Bureau, went further in his promises to the farming population. In April 1931 he wrote in the *Völkischer Beobachter*: 'We must plan and prepare for a political organisation which will make the farmers the cornerstone in the new state', and argued that farmers needed special protection as guardians of Germany's bloodstock. However, he remained very careful to differentiate the NSDAP from the agrarian special interest parties, or any other Weimar party.
Extracted from Barbara Miller Lane and Leila J. Rupp (eds.), *Nazi Ideology before 1933. A Documentation*, Manchester, 1978, pp. 133–4.

To build up the state as an organism means to affirm the idea of blood and soil: recognition of the significance of blood taught us to respect the soil again. But this recognition necessitates a fundamental renunciation of the prevailing Liberal-Marxist conception of the state. It can be said that the idea of blood and soil presents the German people with an ideological decision of the most fundamental kind. This is the meaning of our era!

Thus far one single political party has not only clearly recognised these relationships, but has also had the courage to set the rudder of its will in the direction of an organic idea of the state and to accept the consequences whatever the cost: this is the movement of Adolf Hitler.

This fact alone suffices to show that there can be no more senseless charge (it is often made!) against this party than that it is hostile to peasants and agriculture.

On the other hand we realise that the idea of blood and soil – it sounds like a contradiction and yet it is not – shows the current call for a 'GREEN FRONT' to be fallacious. The previous development of the Liberal-Marxist state brought German agriculture to its present desperate condition, because agriculture in relation to other occupational groups will never be able to hold its own for long in a state based on purely economic considerations.

Versailles-Dawes-Young has accelerated the present condition of German agriculture but is not its sole cause. Not only agriculture is going under at present, but practically everything GERMAN. To form a 'GREEN FRONT' today is as reasonable as trying to set up trade unions on a sinking ship in order, while the ship sinks, to secure the best possible economic rights for each occupational group among the crew.

What we need now is not a 'Green Front' but a 'German Front', which first and foremost will save Germandom from going under, and will erect a state in which the German can feel at home. Adolf Hitler has recognised this task and the secret of his success lies in his ability to see it through consistently and persuasively.

Document 22
Gregor Strasser's parliamentary speech: 'Work and Bread!'

In May 1932 Strasser presented to the Reichstag his proposals for creating and funding a full employment programme. His language and imagery were altogether less mystical than Darré's, but it is telling that he, too, set the theme of job creation in a wide social and economic context, discussing, *inter alia*, agrarian reform and that he, too, condemned the pluralistic parliamentary system.

Extracted from: Barbara Miller Lane and Leila J. Rupp (eds.), *Nazi Ideology before 1933. A Documentation*, Manchester, 1978, pp. 137–45.

We have said for years that the following problems are at issue in Germany: the improvement of the economic situation of the farmers – I say explicitly the farmers; the necessity of internal resettlement; the reduction of migration to the city; the recovery of trade and the monetary system; the increase of domestic production, which goes hand in hand with support for an autarkic economy; assurance of an adequate food supply; the organisation of national labour; the establishment of a domestically-based market with the co-operation of industry; the revision of our land law; and, perhaps the most important, the proclamation of what I call the duty to work and the duty to provide food, that is, the obligation of the German ethnic comrade to devote all of his labour to the nation in the production of necessities. We demand the assessment and valuation of the individual according to the extent of his realised achievements. Whether he works as a privy councillor or as an unskilled labourer is of no consequence.

. . . Article 163 of the constitution, which regulates the right to work, must be complemented by the second demand which I formulated earlier as the obligation to work, the utilisation of labour for the general public. From labour comes life's necessities: food, housing, clothing, light and warmth. Labour, not capital is the wealth of a people; everything stems from labour. Therefore, when confronting the problem of the provision of employment, the state must never ask, 'Is there money for it?'. There is only one single question to be asked: 'How should the money be used?'.

. . . We will have to realise that in all [our] new employment plans one conception must be completely discarded: the capitalist calculation of profit. We must not ask how much of this labour will produce interest to fatten the coffers of the money-lender so that he need not work. Rather we should consider what I like to call the National Socialist calculation of profit, in which one looks at the financing of such works from the point of view of the welfare of the entire nation; in which one asks what will be achieved for the economic, cultural and other needs of the whole people.

. . . Chancellor Brüning has certainly approached all these problems with good will; we have never doubted it.

But it seems to me that it was impossible to solve them as long as the leader of the government had to use up all his strength in dealing with those heterogeneous parties which are called a government. I consider it impossible in the long run to govern with a multitude of parties, and above all it is impossible to solve problems. For this reason the 'voters' revolution' as it is often called, which we are experiencing today, is right. Small parties [make] demands in inverse ratio to their size; demands which, because of their internal weakness and because of the immoral position they adopt by remaining [in Parliament] when they no longer have any support outside, are subject to all kinds of corrupting influences. With these one cannot govern; they have to disappear, there is no doubt about it . . .

To a large extent, the German people have earned Adolf Hitler and his movement. We have gained for ourselves the task of governing by building up this movement out of nothing, against you all. The Lord may grant us fulfilment; we leave judgement to history.

Propaganda

The National Socialists were acknowledged experts when it came to propaganda. The meeting and the spoken word were the key vehicles for disseminating the Nazi message and a great deal of care and effort was put into staging meetings and ensuring the effectiveness of speakers.

Document 23
Hitler emphasises the power of the spoken word

Hitler mocked the efforts of intellectuals to pursue political objectives with the pen. Here he evokes the power and emotional pull of the spoken word, making an interesting comparison between Lloyd George and Bethmann-Hollweg who was Chancellor of Germany between 1909 and 1917.

From: A. Hitler, *Mein Kampf (My Struggle)*, London, 1938, pp. 190–2.

It is all one with the silly ignorance of the world shown by our German intelligentsia that they believe that a writer is bound to be an orator's superior in intellect. This view is most delightfully illustrated in an article in a certain Nationalist paper, in which it is stated that one is so often disillusioned on seeing a speech by some admittedly great orator in print. I recollect another article which came into my hands during the War; it seized upon the speeches of Lloyd George, then Minister of Munitions, examined them as under a microscope, only to come to the brilliant conclusion that those speeches showed inferiority of intellect and knowledge, and

151

were otherwise banal and commonplace. I obtained some of those speeches bound in a small volume, and had to laugh out loud at the thought that an ordinary German quill-driver failed to see the point of those psychological masterpieces in the way of influencing the public. The fellow judged the speeches solely by the impression they made on his blasé intellect, whereas the great British demagogue had been able to produce an immense effect by their aid on his audiences, and in the widest sense on the whole of the British lower classes. From this point of view, that Welshman's speeches were most wonderful achievements, for they evinced amazing knowledge of the mentality of the populace; their penetrative effect was decisive in the truest sense.

Compare them with the futile stutterings of Bethmann-Hollweg, whose speeches may have been more intellectual, but really they merely proved the man's inability to speak to his nation.

Lloyd George proved his equality, nay, his immeasurable superiority to Bethmann-Hollweg by the fact that the form and expression of his speeches were such as to open the hearts of his people to him and to make them pay active obedience to his will. The very primitiveness of those speeches, their form of expression, and his choice of easily understood, simple illustration, are proofs of that Welshman's towering political capacity.

Document 24
Hitler explains the purpose of the mass meeting

Hitler understood the emotional forces unleashed at mass meetings better than most and appreciated their importance for the growth of the Nazi movement.
From: A. Hitler, *Mein Kampf (My Struggle)*, London, 1938, pp. 191–2.

Mass assemblies are necessary because whilst attending them the individual who feels on the point of joining a young Movement and takes alarm if left by himself receives his first impression of a larger community, and this has a strengthening and encouraging effect on most people. He submits himself to the magic influence of what we call 'mass-suggestion'. The desires, longings and indeed the strength of thousands is accumulated in the mind of each individual present. A man who enters such a meeting in doubt and hestitation leaves it inwardly fortified; he has become a member of a community. The National Socialist movement may never ignore this.

Document 25
The slide show as propaganda

In April 1929 the *Völkischer Beobachter* (No. 80) advertised two slide-illustrated lectures on offer from Hoffmann Photography in Munich.

DOES YOUR LOCAL BRANCH POSSESS THE ORIGINAL SLIDE-ILLUSTRATED LECTURE YET?

The Soviet Republic in Munich, 1919

with 70 slides, 8½ × 8½ cm, on the events and personalities of the Jewish Government in Bavaria. It was ten years ago that a horde of criminals under Jewish leadership tyrannised an entire people. It is of enormous value for we National Socialists that this rare material is made accessible to the general public. In addition I have put together a slide-illustrated lecture:

The Struggle and Development of the NSDAP

70 original exposures demonstrate the powerful development of our Movement. The mass parades are a documentary record which should without question be exploited by us as propaganda!

Hoffmann Photography/Munich/Schellingstrasse 50

Document 26
The NSDAP trains its public speakers

The Nazi movement trained its public speakers with some care as it strove to build up its membership and maximise its vote. Lacking a body of traditional support, the Nazis had to persuade people to change sides or take an interest in politics for the first time. Here the police describe the *modus operandi* of the NSDAP's Speakers' School.

From: Bayerisches Hauptstaatsarchiv Munich, Abt I, So I/1529; Reports of the [Prussian] State Criminal Police (IA) Berlin, 1 June 1930, No. 11.

The National Socialist Speakers' School, which operates under the direction of Gauführer Fritz Reinhardt in Herrsching near Munich, has been officially recognised by the NSDAP since 1 June 1929. There has recently been intensified publicity for it in order to make good the shortage of competent speakers, particularly for meetings in smaller towns and villages.

The training of speakers is accomplished by correspondence

course in the form of monthly instruction packages. The participants are assigned a monthly study programme each time, including guidelines on the preparation of talks. In addition the students are provided with completed lectures and are expected to prepare commentaries on their contents. The answers which they send in are appraised by the School's staff and returned with sample commentaries.

A participant at the Speakers' School is only finally recognised as an official Party Speaker after participating in the correspondence course for 12 months and speaking publicly thirty times within 8 months.

This year it is planned to hold a further, oral course in Herrsching. The precondition for attendance is a minimum of 6 months' satisfactory participation on the correspondence course.

Participation in the Speakers' School is open to every member of the NSDAP upon payment of the appropriate fee.

Speakers in possession of a 'Certificate of Aptitude' are permitted to hold local training evenings at which they can train speakers according to the methods of the Speakers' School. . . .

Document 27
The content of Nazi propaganda

What subject matter did courses at the Speakers' School actually include? How were the oral courses organised? The programme for one such, held in August 1931 is set out below. Note the importance of some of the speakers within the National Socialist movement and the surprising breadth of the topics covered.

From: Bayerisches Hauptstaatsarchiv Munich, Abt I, SO I/1529; Files of the Munich Police, 17 August 1931.

Schedule of the Oral Course held by the National Propaganda Directorate II in Herrsching from 17 to 31 August inclusive.
Monday 17 August
09.00 – 10.00 **Reinhardt**: Introduction
10.00 – 12.00 **Reinhardt**: Tribute, Currency and Economy
13.30 – 16.30 **Oberlindober**: National Socialism and Support for War Victims
17.00 – 19.00 **Reinhardt**: Tribute, Currency and Economy (Continuation and Conclusion)

Tuesday 18 August
09.00 – 12.00& **Dr Wagener**, Chief of the Economic Policy

13.00 – 16.00 Section of the National Directorate: National Socialist Economic Policy

Wednesday 19 August
09.30 – 13.00 **Dr von Renteln**, Specialist in the Economic Policy Section of the National Directorate: Work and the Shaping of Life (Social Policy)

Thursday 20 August
09.30 – 13.00 **Julius Streicher**: The Jewish Question
20.00 – 23.00 **Plenary Session**. Speaker: Julius Streicher

Friday 21 August
15.00 – 18.30 **Walther Schuhmann**, Leader of the National Factory Cell Organisation: Meaning and Growth of the NSDAP's National Factory Cell Organisation

Saturday 22 August
09.30 – 11.30 **Dr Konopath**, Chief of the Cultural Policy Section of the National Directorate: Blood and Race in the German Nation
15.00 – 18.30 **Town Councillor Fiehler**, Specialist in Community Politics Issues within the National Directorate: National Socialist Community Politics
20.00 – 22.30 **Plenary Session**. Speaker: Dr Konopath

Sunday 23 August
07.30 – 10.00 **Reinhardt**: The National Socialists in the Reichstag; the others and us
10.30 – 12.00 **Alfred Rosenberg**: National Socialist Foreign Policy
14.00 – 15.30 **Alfred Rosenberg**: The Militant League for German Culture
16.00 – 18.00 **Walter Darré**, Chief of the Agricultural Policy Section of the National Directorate: National Socialist Agricultural Policy

Monday 24 August
09.30 – 13.00 **Dr Lorenz**, Specialist in the Economic Policy Section of the National Directorate: Marxism
15.00 – 18.00 **Karl Röwer**, Leader of the National Socialists in Oldenburg: National Socialism in Oldenburg and the Oldenburg State Parliament

Tuesday 25 August ⎫
Wednesday 26 August ⎬
Whichever of these days sees good weather will be kept free to allow the Party Comrades time to participate in a long-distance

tour of the Bavarian High Alps (Garmisch-Partenkirchen, Kochel, Tegernsee, Mittenwald, Zugspitze, Füssen, Tirol etc) starting from Herrsching on the day in question. On the other of the two days:

08.00 – 12.00 **Reinhardt**: Our Weapons and our Offensive against the different Parties

16.00 – 19.00 **Georg Sturm**, Leader of the Action Group against Department Stores and Cooperatives, *Gau* Munich– Upper Bavaria: Department Stores, Cooperatives and National Socialism

Thursday 27 August

09.30 – 13.00 **Dr Frank** II: National Socialism's View of the Law

15.00 – 19.00 **Reinhardt**: The Law for the Protection of the Republic of 25 March 1930 and the Emergency Decrees against 'Political Disturbances' of 28 March and 17 July 1931

Friday 28 August

09.30 – 11.30 **Kurt Gruber**, National Chief of the Hitler Youth: Meaning, Organisation and Growth of the Hitler Youth

14.00 – 16.00 SA Leader (Speaker not yet confirmed): Meaning, Organisation and Growth of the SA

16.00 – 18.00 **Himmler**, National Chief of the SS: Meaning, Organisation and Growth of the SS.

Saturday 29 August

10.00 – 13.00 **Gottfried Feder**: The Destruction of Interest Slavery

14.00 – 17.30 **Dr Buttmann**: The National Socialist View of the State

Sunday 30 August

09.30 – 13.00 **Dr Buttmann**: National Socialist Educational and Religious Policy

14.00 – 16.30 **Martin Mutschmann**, Leader of the National Socialists in Saxony: Our Activities in Saxony and in the Saxon State Parliament

Monday 31 August

09.30 – 13.00 **Colonel Hierl**: National Socialist Military Policy

15.00 – 18.00 **Reinhardt**: Concluding Lecture

Right reserved to alter or add to the lecture schedule. Additional lectures will be given by me and incorporated in the teaching programme on days when the weather is bad.

Leader of the Course   Signed: Fritz Reinhardt

Political violence

Violence was one of the hallmarks of Nazi politics. The movement's leaders condoned or encouraged it, the police struggled to
control it, political rivals often responded in kind but were not
always sure of what to make of it.

Document 28
Adolf Hitler

Writing in the SA's newspaper several weeks before his appointment as Chancellor, Hitler advocated the pursuit of political
violence briefly and succinctly.
From: A. Hitler, 'Das Braune Heer' in *Der SA-Mann*, 2(1), 7 January 1933,
p. 1.

> Because terror is the main weapon of Marxist struggle, we cannot
> retreat back into the salon, mouthing idiotic, bourgeois, legalistic
> platitudes, or hope for help from the state. Instead we have to
> confront Marxism bravely, in order to destroy it. . . .

Document 29
A violent meeting

In fact brawls, intimidation and fear were typical of late Weimar
politics. Here, as the police report, a Communist meeting is
wrecked by the Nazis.
From: Staatsarchiv Bremen 4,65/1268/211. Police Headquarters, Munich.
Extract from the Situation Briefing of 12 September 1929.

> On 6 February 1929 the founding meeting of the Antifascist
> Defence League Munich-East was scheduled for the Stadtkeller in
> Munich. Promotional publicity included anti-Nazi leaflets. Com-
> munists and National Socialists appeared at the meeting in equal
> strength. When the singing of a song with the words 'Hitler is our
> Leader' was followed by shouts of 'Heil Moscow', the two parties
> set upon each other with beer mugs, seats, plates, carpenter's
> nails, knives, steel rods, rubber coshes and the like. Police on hand
> cleared the room. Eight people were injured, two seriously. Two
> police officers also needed attention.

Document 30
A climate of intimidation and fear in Saxony

The police had some success in containing major acts of violence, but could not stamp out the incessant outbreaks of petty intimidation.

From: Staatsarchiv Bremen, 4,65/256/48. Extract from the Situation Report of the Free State of Saxony of 24 October 1931. I. General Developments.

Thanks to comprehensive police measures at all political functions there have been no noteworthy incidents – in particular fights or brawls – on any significant scale. However, one has to observe that the confrontational attitude adopted by political parties to one another finds expression in numerous skirmishes and tiffs, above all between the NSDAP and KPD. Surprise attacks on individual persons, generally at night and invariably when the police are not in the vicinity, are proliferating. Incoming reports on bodily harm, violent assault and the like lead to the conclusion that in most cases the attacks are on National Socialists and – in as far as perpetrators can be identified – the attackers are Communists.

The NSDAP and KPD have also pursued very active recruitment drives and held many meetings during the period covered by this report.

Document 31
Nazi terror in Brunswick

By April 1932 the NSDAP had entered government in the State of Brunswick. For the Nazis' Communist and Social Democratic opponents the consequences were disastrous, as a Communist official reported to his Central Committee.

From: Bundesarchiv Koblenz R45IV/25. Signed Adolf Benscheid, Brunswick, 29 April 1932. To the Political Secretariat of the KPD's Central Committee.

The strength of the Nazis is sufficiently well known to make it enough here to concentrate on matters of detail. The fascists, who are protected by state power, are unleashing terror on a scale which has no parallel elsewhere in Germany – with the exception of Schleswig-Holstein. Even in the city of Brunswick there are streets in which our comrades hardly dare be seen after dark. A Brunswick comrade told me that once it got dark he and his family could only leave or enter their house in disguise. The police pay no attention at all to these occurrences and avoid confrontation with the Nazis, even if they do not directly support these murderous bandits. The Klagges [Minister President of Brunswick] Government would dismiss at once any police officer who acted against these bandits. There are without doubt still SPD supporters in the police ranks in relatively large measure, but even they do not attempt simply to protect their own supporters – SPD workers or Reichsbanner workers. In the countryside things are even worse.

Document 32
The Social Democrats condemn the radical extremes

The two main radical movements, the National Socialists and Communists, attracted many supporters who were anti-Weimar rather than Nazi or Communist in any positive sense. They could switch from one extreme to the other if needs be. The main republican party, the SPD, noted this common negative bond with some bitterness – as in this particular newspaper report. However, the Social Democrats exaggerated the extent of transfers between the radical extremes and in electoral terms at least the SPD lost many more supporters to the Nazis than did the Communists.

'Hakenstern und Sowjetkreuz' (Hooked Star and Soviet Cross), *Bremer Volkszeitung*, 67, 20 March 1931.

Through toying with illegality the KPD attracts all sorts of shady elements into its ranks who, at the first opportunity and in particular in return for payment, go over at once to the Nazis, there to betray their knowledge of the Communist movement . . . It is clear that a not inconsiderable proportion of former Red Front functionaries are active today as regimental and company leaders of the Nazi SA and SS . . .

On the other hand National Socialists transfer with the same ease to the Communists . . . All these examples show how extraordinarily fluid the boundaries are between the parties of the two alleged 'extremes'. Nazis and Kozis share the same methods of political rowdyism, they share a common romantic-reactionary/revolutionary ideology, they have the same enemy – Social Democracy – and it is clear that many National Socialist members are strongly anti-capitalist. With so many points of contact it is understandable that members surge back and forth between the two parties.

Document 33
A Communist view of working-class Nazism

In the autumn of 1932 the KPD observed that it was not Hitler and his lieutenants in person who were attacking the organised left. The SA, above all others, was doing that, but there was a need to distinguish between the instigators and executors of violence, to understand the latter without excusing them.

From: Bundesarchiv Koblenz R45IV/39. 'Schluss mit dem SA Terror', *Red Aid of Germany*, 2, 'The Real Guilty Parties', pp. 4–5.

These others have no bank account and no salary; most have no job. They suffer from starvation every bit as much as the other workers. For sure they receive the occasional beer, a couple of cigarettes, food from soup kitchens, sometimes even a Mark or two (excluding the exceptional cases of outright bribery). But they scarcely act for these reasons. They storm into the working-class areas, they provoke clashes and pursue their bloody and murderous trade because they believe that this will help to establish the Third Reich; a Reich which will provide them – who are without work or hope – with work and bread.

The fact that over a hundred thousand proletarian lads give themselves over to such deeds, that their natural activity and activism are used against their own class, is a sign of the unspeakable deprivation into which the ruling class has pitched working youth.

Among the SA proletarians in particular one finds young men who have never worked in the production process because as they finished with school there was no factory, no workshop to admit them, who became caught up in family conflicts at home, because the father was usually out of work himself. Finally, because they couldn't conceive of any other escape they fell into the clutches of that organisation [the SA] which trained them to kill workers and intoxicated them with the fraud of the Third Reich.

Organisation

The National Socialists had to throw together an effective organisation at very short notice in order to sustain a massive political offensive against the Weimar Republic. Hitler wrote at times that it would be best to restrict recruitment to the party so as to maintain its quality, but in reality over a million Germans joined the wider Nazi movement.

Document 34
Hitler condemns coalitions and compromise

Hitler argued in *Mein Kampf* that the single most effective and capable national movement should prevail absolutely. He saw no future in coalitions or collaboration, except in the short term for opportunistic reasons. As his conservative political allies were later to discover, he meant what he said.
From: A. Hitler, *Mein Kampf (My Struggle)*, London, 1938, p. 206.

> It ought never to be forgotten that no really great achievement has ever been effected in this world by coalitions; instead they have always been due to the triumph of one individual man. Successes achieved by coalition, owing to the nature of their source, contain the seeds of future disintegration from their very start, to the extent, indeed, of forfeiting what has been attained up to that point. Great alterations of thought which really revolutionise the world are inconceivable and unrealisable except in the form of titanic struggles conducted by single forces – never in the form of enterprises conducted by coalitions.
>
> The national state, therefore, will never be created by the unstable volition of a nationalist confederation of workers, but only by the adamantine will-power of a single movement, after that movement has won through, having defeated all others.

Document 35
Hitler on the origins of the leader principle

In 1921 Hitler became leader of the NSDAP on terms which gave him absolute authority over its affairs. It became a principle of National Socialism that authority be vested in the person of the leader (*Führer*) and then delegated by him down through the movement's hierarchy.
From: A. Hitler, *Mein Kampf (My Struggle)*, London, 1938, pp. 234–5.

> As controller of propaganda for the party I was careful not merely to prepare the ground for the future greatness of the movement, but I worked on very radical principles so that only the best material was introduced into the organisation. For the more radical and exciting my propaganda was, the more did it frighten weak and wavering characters away, and prevented their penetrating into the inner kernel of our organisation. And this was all to the good.

Up to the middle of 1921 this creative activity sufficed, and did nothing but good to the movement. But in the summer of that year certain events made it obvious that the organisation was failing to keep pace with the propaganda, the success of which was gradually appearing more evident.

In the years 1920-21 the movement had a committee in control of it, elected by the members in assembly. This committee, comically enough, embodied the very principle against which the movement was most keenly fighting, namely, parliamentarianism.

I refused to countenance such folly, and after a very short time I ceased to attend the meetings of the committee. I made my propaganda as I wished, and that was an end of it; I refused to allow any ignoramus to talk me into any other course. Similarly I refrained from interfering with the others in their departments.

As soon as the new rules were adopted and I was established as Chairman of the party, thus acquiring the necessary authority and the rights accompanying it, all such folly came to an immediate end. Decisions by committee were replaced by the principle of absolute responsibility. The chairman is responsible for entire control of the movement.

This principle gradually became recognised inside the movement as the natural one, at least as far as control of the party was concerned.

Document 36
The funding of the Nazi movement

How did the Nazi movement sustain itself financially? It was once supposed that mysterious, wealthy backers must have bankrolled the burgeoning movement, but convincing evidence was never produced and there is now a consensus that the National Socialists in essence funded themselves from the grass roots. The annual accounts of the East Prussian party branch of Preussisch Holland give an insight into the nature of this grass-roots funding. Note how monies raised were in significant measure passed on by the branch to the centre, or spent on activities of other sections of the Nazi movement, such as the SA.

From: Staatliches Archivlager Göttingen, Rep. 240 C71b.

Report to the 1930 Accounts of the Town Group in Preussisch Holland, East Prussia

Preussisch Holland, 08.3.1931

Receipts		**Expenditure**	
I. Subscriptions		*I. Subscriptions*	
a) Adoption Dues	100.00	Adoption Dues	104.50
b) Monthly Dues	337.90	Monthly Dues	343.55
c) Publicity Fees	45.90	Publicity Fees	—.—
d) Documentation Fees	—.—	Documentation Fees	—.—
e) SA Insurance Dues	132.30	SA Insurance Dues	170.40
f) Extraordinary Dues	—.—	Extraordinary Dues	—.—
II. Donations		*II. Administrative Expenses*	
a) Voluntary and from Collections	1620.68	a) Town Group	299.37
		b) District Leader	108.20
		c) SA Lieutenant & Colonel	61.40
III. Propaganda		*III. Propaganda*	
a) Sale of Admission Tickets to Meetings	1203.65	a) Small Ads, Leaflets Speakers' Fees	1352.10
b) Donations to the Fighting Fund, resp. Meetings	754.05	b) Travel, local SA	413.25
		c) Travel, outside SA	88.00
		d) Rent for Rooms	196.30
		e) Donations to Gau resp. Elections	200.00
IV. General		*IV. Extraordinary Expenses*	
	475.95	a) For local SA	771.96
		b) For Hitler Youth	22.20
		c) Cover for Damages at Meeting 12.3.30	102.45
		V. General	
			298.50
	4670.43		4532.18

Signed: Gerull, 1st Auditor
Signed: Wenk, 2nd Auditor

Document 37
Financial help from wealthy citizens

The NSDAP had sympathisers who were well placed in German society, preferred not to join the party, but were prepared to give discreet assistance. The Nazi movement organised them accordingly, although this particular group only lasted for slightly over a year.
From: Staatliches Archivlager Göttingen, Rep. 240 A5d, Files of the Prussian State Police of 15 February 1930.

The German Women's Order has recently established a 'Charitable Circle of the German Women's Order' which, so far, has been joined by 100 persons of both sexes. They are prosperous people who are to support the overall movement through donations. Members of the Charitable Circle need not belong to the NSDAP.

Welfare

The National Socialist movement organised a substantial welfare effort at the end of the Weimar era. Members of Nazi organisations could reasonably expect a measure of help for themselves and their families from the movement if they were in need, although the Nazis were never in a position to satisfy adequately the welfare needs of all their constituents. It was in the realm of welfare that female members of the Nazi movement played their one major function.

Document 38
The role of the Women's Action Committee

The activities of the Berlin group in 1930 were typical of the Nazis' welfare effort which, apart from producing concrete results gave the appearance of considerable effort and commitment.
From: Staatliches Archivlager Göttingen. Rep. 240 A5d. Report of the Prussian State Police Office, Berlin, 15 November 1930.

The Women's Action Committee of the NSDAP's Greater Berlin Region has been increasingly active on behalf of the movement. During the election campaign foodstuffs were efficiently collected and distributed to the SA members while they were on duty. In various SA pubs hot meals were actually prepared and distributed to SA members. Even after the election campaign this provisioning was continued for longer-serving SA members in the larger units. During the metal workers' strike the Women's Action Committee distributed all their available food supplies to the striking party members, prepared hot meals and fed the unmarried party members who were on strike three times daily in their local SA pub.

The Women's Action Committee has recently concentrated more on collecting cash donations so as to sustain the purchase of foodstuffs. However, in the countryside foodstuffs are to be collected in still greater measure from farmers, so that the money collected can be used to obtain clothing for the approaching winter. When collecting from tradesmen a questionnaire entitled 'German Tradesmen' is handed out for completion. Usually they wish in this way to get the tradesman to make a donation on the spot.

Document 39
Who joined the Women's Groups?

Relatively little is known about the membership of the Women's Groups, but as a report of 7 March 1931 from Gumbinnen, East Prussia shows, they could embrace women from the entire local community. Their involvement in supportive and charitable work in this way is precisely what Nazi ideology expected of women. Here an external speaker is requested to educate the local group.
From: Staatliches Archivlager Göttingen, Rep. 240 C48b.

The Women's Group in Gumbinnen is composed of all sections of the population; senior, middle-ranking and junior civil servants' wives, tradesmen's wives and workers' wives. The last comprise 50% of the group. I regard it as very important and advantageous that the female Party Comrade speaks here in Gumbinnen and enlightens the Women's Group in politics and ideology. . . .

G. Dettmer
District Leader

Document 40
Gregor Strasser sets guidelines for welfare work

Party Headquarters in Munich recognised the importance of welfare work and set guidelines accordingly. However, the

centre lacked the means to fund such a programme. Responsibility was devolved to the regions and to particular organisations.
From: Staatliches Archivlager Göttingen. Rep. 240 A5d. *Verordnungsblatt der Reichsleitung der Nationalsozialistischen Deutschen Arbeiterpartei*, No 11, Munich, 16 November 1931.

Announcement
It is planned in the future to establish an independent, officially-recognised nursing organisation to carry out medical work - the 'Red Swastika'; however at present medical training should be given within the individual women's groups. (First aid courses by National Socialist doctors). District Party Leaders, in association with the SA Commanders and the Women's Leaders are responsible for undertaking everything possible during the coming winter to ameliorate want and suffering within the individual Party Branches. The *Gau* or, in addition, the District is to have primary responsibility for obtaining the resources for relief work.

Document 41
No central finance for hostels

Even before Gregor Strasser's announcement, Party Headquarters in Munich had made it plain that the welfare effort had to be funded on the spot.
From: Staatliches Archivlager Göttingen, Rep. 240 C37e.

To Gau Commissar 15
Party Comrade Dr Knabe
Friedrichshof   15 May 1931
As you know the National Directorate refuses to give support of any kind to SA or Hitler Hostels. The East Prussian Regional Directorate adopts the same standpoint. The Hitler Hostel in Johannisburg is therefore to be supported by the Party Branch in Johannisburg. The Branch Leader and the Gau Commissar must take on all obligations regarding this hostel.
                                              Signed
                                              Director of Organisation I

Document 42
The NSBO and the welfare effort

Almost every Nazi organisation contributed to the welfare effort. Here a newspaper report describes a Christmas party organised in 1932 by the NSBO's Railways Group in Munich.

Selected documents

From: 'Weihnachten unterm Hakenkreuz', *Völkischer Beobachter*, 355, 20 December 1932.

On 10 December the Railways Group (workers and staff) held their first Christmas party in the 'Friedenheimer Garden' SA Hostel. Despite the railway personnel's extremely difficult economic circumstances the party was very well attended and the tireless leader, N. Berger, as well as his shop stewards, put on an excellent programme . . .

Our dear little kids were amply provided for with food and toys. The Group also remembered their many unemployed colleagues and knew how to give them an enjoyable evening.

Document 43
The SA and the welfare effort

The SA also played a vital part in the Nazis' welfare effort, particularly among the unemployed. Their own members received assistance, and SA hostels and pubs were used as distribution centres and meeting places by other parts of the Nazi movement.

From: 'Weihnachtsfeier der Standarte R16 "List" München', *Der SA-Mann*, No. 38, 31 December 1932.

Lastly it should be mentioned that at Christmas each SA Company gifted a total of about 150 unemployed with food and cash. The distribution of Christmas presents to children was carried out in liaison with the Political Executive.

Document 44
A Nazi charity collection

The Protestant rural population often sympathised strongly with National Socialism by the early 1930s. Quite substantial amounts of foodstuffs and old clothing could be collected door to door in the countryside for distribution to needy supporters, here in East Prussia.

From: Staatliches Archivlager Göttingen, Rep. 240 C49e.

NSDAP
Bladiau Party Branch   7 December 1931

Sunday 15 November to Monday 30 November: Collection for the
SA Winter Relief Programme. Collected in the period:

35 cwt of grain	3 boys' smocks
17.5 cwt of potatoes	2 windcheater jackets
6 cwt of white cabbage	3 pairs of trousers
1 cwt of peas	1 shirt
1 cwt of rice	2 pairs of socks
1 cwt of rye flour	1 pair of shoes
25 lb of [illegible]	3 caps
5 lb of porridge oats	1 [illegible]
5 lb of semolina	

The Nazi constituency

Once regarded as predominantly lower-middle-class, the
NSDAP's constituency has now been characterised as particularly diverse in social terms.

Document 45
The NSDAP

Detlef Mühlberger's findings, as set out below, demonstrate just
how socially diverse the Nazi Party's membership was. His overall conclusion, that the NSDAP was over 40 per cent working-
class, has now been confirmed by Jürgen Falter among others. In
comparison with the 'Total' figures below, the 1925 census indicated that 53.7 per cent of the male working population was
working-class, 46.3 per cent was middle- and upper-class.

Adapted from: D. Mühlberger, 'A "Workers' Party" or a "Party without Workers" . . .', in C. Fischer (ed.), *Weimar, the Working Classes and the Rise of National Socialism*, Oxford, 1995, forthcoming.

The social structure of the membership of the NSDAP in various regions of Germany, 1925 – 31.1.1933 (%)

Region	Lower class	Lower & middle middle class	Upper middle class & upper class	Status unknown	Total
Western Ruhr	50.8	38.3	1.0	6.5	100
Gau Hanover-South-Brunswick	37.1	45.5	5.4	11.9	100
Gau Hesse-Darmstadt	39.4	50.1	4.0	6.5	100
Gau Württemberg-Hohenzollern	42.9	46.3	5.4	5.4	100
Gau Hesse-Nassau-South	41.6	45.5	4.3	8.6	100
Grenzmark Posen-West Prussia	37.6	48.4	3.2	10.8	100
Total (*N*: 52,579)	41.9	45.9	4.6	7.6	100

Western Ruhr: 1925–26; *N*: 874
Gau Hanover–South–Brunswick: 1925–30.1.1933; *N*: 2,089
Gau Hesse–Darmstadt: 1925–30.1.1933; *N*: 2,614
Gau Württemberg–Hohenzollern: 1928–1930/32; *N*: 17,636
Gau Hessen–Nassau–South: 1929–30.1.1933; *N*: 28,903
Grenzmark Posen–West Prussia: 1930–31; *N*: 463

Document 46
The SA

The SA's members were recruited largely from among the younger, male unemployed population of Germany. Most were workers, the apparent variations between the pre- and post-January 1933 periods are the result of variations in sources available. Controlling for this, for gender and for age, it emerges that the SA appealed most strongly to workers, salaried staff and, after 1933, also to young civil servants.

Selected documents

From: C. Fischer and D. Mühlberger, 'The Pattern of the SA's Social Appeal', in C. Fischer (ed.), *Weimar, the Working Classes and the Rise of National Socialism*, Oxford, 1995, forthcoming.

The German SA (%)

Class	Occupational group	1925 to Jan. 1933	Feb. 1933 to Jun. 1934
Working classes	Agricultural	2.9	6.0
	Unskilled	15.4	21.8
	Skilled	35.4	36.7
	Public sector	0.9	1.2
	Apprentices	1.5	0.5
	Servants	0.4	0.1
Subtotal		**56.5**	**66.3**
Lower middle & middle classes	Master artisans	1.3	1.6
	Non-grad. professions	3.3	1.4
	Salaried staff	8.8	7.3
	Civil servants	2.7	4.6
	Soldiers & NCOs	0.0	0.0
	Salesmen/merchants	10.4	5.9
	Farmers	4.3	2.8
	Family helpers	2.1	1.1
Subtotal		**32.9**	**24.7**
Upper middle & upper classes	Senior salaried staff	0.2	0.2
	Senior civil servants	0.1	0.5
	Military officers	0.0	0.0
	University students	4.1	1.4
	Graduate professions	1.2	2.3
	Entrepreneurs	0.2	0.3
Subtotal		**5.8**	**4.7**
Unclear	Schoolboys/students	1.9	3.3
	Retired	0.4	0.1
	Others/no info.	2.0	0.7
Subtotal		**4.3**	**4.1**
Total		**100.0**	**100.0**
(Numbers		2,643	2,356)

Document 47
The electorate

In 1991 the political scientist Jürgen Falter summarised the results of years of complex, computer-driven investigation into the NSDAP's electoral base as follows.

Adapted from J. W. Falter, 'War die NSDAP die erste deutsche Volkspartei?', in M. Prinz and R. Zitelmann (eds), *Nationalsozialismus und Modernisierung*, Darmstadt, 1991, p. 42.

The social composition of the Nazi electorate (%)

Election	1928	1930	1932Jul	1932Nov	1933
Denomination					
Catholic	30	20	17	17	24
Other or none	70	80	83	83	76
Community Size[a]					
0–5000	39	41	45	47	47
5000–20000	14	13	13	12	12
20000–100000	16	15	13	13	13
>100000	31	31	28	27	28
Social Group[a]					
Workers	40	40	39	39	40
Salaried/civil servants	22	21	19	19	18
Independents & farmers	37	39	42	41	42
% of total electorate voting NS[b]	2	15	31	27	39

[a] By way of comparison 42% of the population lived in communities of <5000, 13% 5000–20000, 14% 20000–100000, 31% >100000. According to the 1925 census, the population was 45.1% working-class, 21.4% salaried staff and civil servants and 34.5% independents, farmers, and their immediate family members.

[b] N.B. This is a proportion of the total registered electorate rather than of those who actually voted (typically around 80%).

National Socialism and the middle classes

The National Socialists fared extraordinarily well in Protestant middle-class Germany, so much so that Nazism was often characterised in the past as a lower middle-class movement. Protestant farmers, tradesmen, civil servants and, to a degree, salaried staff

Selected documents

provided the Nazis with invaluable electoral support or joined the movement as their traditional parties and professional groups failed to make their mark in the Weimar political system and were unequal to the challenges of the Great Depression.

Document 48
The National Socialists woo the Franconian peasantry

The Nazis enjoyed major successes in Protestant Franconia which lay in north-eastern Bavaria. Here the first signs of their rural offensive are observed in April 1929 by the Communist Reichstag Deputy Johann Meyer.
From: Staatsarchiv Bremen 4,65/249/45. Nr 147/II. Sonderbericht 147/II/29.

> An unmistakeable process of radicalisation has occurred among the peasantry which we must not leave unexploited. The Agricultural Emergency Programme has not helped the peasants, instead favouring the large-scale farmers in the main. The Fascists are becoming very active here as elsewhere. There is a danger that the Fascists may be able to mis-use the peasants for their own purposes. . . .

Document 49
The SA defends farming interests in explosive fashion

As farms went bankrupt the authorities held forced auctions to realise what assets they could. With active or passive connivance from local farming communities the SA launched a campaign of terror across northern Germany in August 1932. For the storm-troopers involved this campaign channelled their disappointment over Hitler's failure to win outright in the July 1932 Reichstag elections.
From: Staatliches Archivlager Göttingen. Rep. 240 B31c. 'Wie kam es nun zum 1. August 1932?', p. 11.

> In the Nordmark (Schleswig-Holstein) the auctioning of farmers' livestock and property was made impossible by the SA.
> Bombs and hand grenades were hurled in self-defence against the Finance Offices which were hounding mercilessly our ethnic comrades from farmhouse and farmland. . . .

172

Document 50
The Saxon middle classes turn to the Nazis

Radical, National Socialist ideology became increasingly attractive to the traditional middle classes as the economic crisis worsened during the early 1930s. In this report the KPD's resentment at Nazi successes is clearly discernible.

From: Bundesarchiv Koblenz, R45IV/16. Report to 1st District Conference of the Saxon KPD, 3 and 4 May 1930, p. 8.

> The National Fascists are trying to exploit the situation in order to gain support, among the working people and especially among the self-employed craftsmen and small farmers who are becoming increasingly proletarianised. The Nazis are deluding the masses with radical slogans on the 'struggle against rapacious capital' and the 'national revolution' and are creating the impression among these groups that they oppose imperialist monopoly capital. Their radical appearance has been providing them with a constantly growing body of support for quite some time.

Document 51
An imminent Nazi breakthrough into bourgeois ranks

After the September 1930 elections the National Socialists were a force to be reckoned with. The KPD's Central Committee feared that the older bourgeois parties were disintegrating and that the Nazis were creating a formidable coalition of workers and the radicalised middle classes. In reality, of course, the Nazis' 'national revolution' was to prove far more credible as a concept for most middle-class and many working-class Germans than was the KPD's 'proletarian revolution'.

From: Staatsarchiv Bremen 4,65/252/46. IAN 2160/6.10.1930.

> The enormous danger posed by the National Socialist movement resides in its success in winning over the working masses who are almost entirely dissatisfied with, and in despair over bourgeois politics; up until now they constituted the support for the bourgeois parties (and to a degree the Social Democrats). Among the millions of Nazi supporters there is no doubt that groups predominate which belong to the proletariat in class terms, are close to the proletariat, or could be won over as allies for the revolutionary proletariat: salaried staff, civil servants, the self-employed, farmers etc.

Document 52
The importance of salaried and civil service supporters

In inter-war Germany officialdom and private citizens had a finely-developed perception of social position. Workers comprised a minority (some 45 per cent) of the employed population, and many employees in relatively humble, often manual, occupations enjoyed salaried or even civil service status. As the economic crisis undermined their standing they were promised renewed advancement by the Nazis or inclusion in a proletarian alliance by the Communists. They preferred the former option.

From: Staatsarchiv Bremen, 4.65/283/56. Z St. 6932/32 geh. KPD District Conference, Weser-Ems, 26 and 27 November 1932, pp. 51–2.

Within the state boundaries of Bremen salaried staff make up over 30 per cent of the economically active population. Looking specifically at the towns, for example Bremen itself or Oldenburg, there are as many, if not more, salaried staff or civil servants than workers. These figures become comprehensible when one notes that Bremen, as a huge trading and port city, possesses a vast army of employees in the offices of the import and export firms, the shipping lines, the tobacco, coffee, wool and dockyard industries, in the banks and the warehouses. In the state of Oldenburg the city, which serves as the seat of government and headquarters of the Oldenburg Railways Executive, possesses state administrative institutions which play a decisive role in employing civil servants who, combined with salaried staff, constitute an overwhelming majority in the town . . .

There is a continual tendency for their living standards to fall to working-class levels resulting in the proletarianisation of large numbers of salaried staff and junior civil servants. This is being cleverly exploited by the Nazis [NSBO].

Document 53
Clerical staff, shop assistants and Nazis

Many clerical staff and shop assistants turned to the Nazis during the early 1930s, but their trade union leaders were altogether more sceptical. Trouble could result, as this report of November 1931 from the NSDAP's District headquarters in Marienburg demonstrates.

From: Staatliches Archivlager Göttingen Rep. 240 C38c2. Geschäftsstelle Marienburg, 12.11.1931.

The Elbing Branch of the German Nationalist Clerical Staff and Shop Assistants' Union [DHV] has recently begun to inveigh vigorously against us. Even so, a large proportion of the members are on our side and some have joined us. The Secretary, however, supports the *völkisch* Conservatives and the Branch Chairman belongs to the Tannenberg League. At the last meeting it was declared that in terms of our programme we were enemies of any form of social policy, were lackeys of capitalism and so on. Then there was trouble. Part of the SA, who are members of the DHV, brought the meeting to a premature end.

Document 54
A middle-class storm-trooper reflects on his misfortunes

Although written in early 1934, this essay shows how severely many young, middle-class Germans and their families were affected by the Great Depression. Although the author was from a Catholic home, and therefore not a typical Nazi supporter, the implicit message here is that the devastation of hopes and ambitions could turn almost any young, male German towards the SA.
From: Nordrhein-Westfälisches Hauptstaatsarchiv Düsseldorf, RW23. Curriculum Vitae of Heinrich R.

I was born on 14 May 1910 in Würselen of Catholic parents. I attended primary school there for seven years from the age of six and then, at the age of 13½ went to the state pre-grammar school, passing my one-year examination at Easter 1928. Following three years' at the state grammar school in Jülich I took my Highers (*Abitur*) at Easter 1931. Because of the financial crisis within my family – my father and three of my siblings had recently lost their jobs – I had to break off my studies. During the following years I tried to obtain a position commensurate with my education, but without success. Only some two years after my school exams was I able to obtain work at the Goulay mine, where I had previously worked frequently during my school holidays. Although the work has absolutely nothing to do with my training, I am none the less happy to be able to support my parents to a degree. My father is still unemployed and my brother only got back to work a couple of weeks ago. What I will achieve professionally and how I shall make use of my acquired skills and knowledge is still not clear to me.

National Socialists and German labour

The National Socialist Movement had a substantial working-class following. Many joined the Nazi Party itself, but two key organisations attracted workers in disproportionate numbers: the Factory Cell Organisation (NSBO) and the SA.

Document 55
The NSBO and the strike question

The NSBO was an active participant in strikes, and its justification for this policy provides revealing insights into wider Nazi thinking. Strikes were seen as an inevitable product of the capitalist economic order; the creation of a harmonious *Volksgemeinschaft* would render them unnecessary once the NSDAP had seized power.

From: Bundesarchiv Koblenz, NS26/1404. Guidelines of the National Factory Cell Executive, Württemberg State Police files, April 1931.

> The strike has become an indispensable weapon in the social struggle for the employee within today's ruling liberal-capitalist economic order. As long as the class contradictions between labour and capital exist and the National Socialist economic order has not been given practical expression, National Socialism accepts the strike as the employee's ultimate weapon. The support for strikes is fundamental and is unaffected by the identity of the instigator, whether Christian, Nationalist, Socialist or the KPD . . .
>
> The aim of the strike is to win improvements in pay or working conditions if these are not granted voluntarily by the employer.
>
> National Socialism is obliged to support such strikes for two sets of reasons: moral and political. The moral obligation is rooted in the fundamental substance and programme of German socialism for which the liberal-capitalist economic system is also an enemy. The political obligation is rooted in the stimulation of resistance against the enslavement of the Young Plan. The employers have officially sanctioned the Young Plan, thereby creating burdens for the economy. It is inherent to an economy which thinks and acts on capitalist lines that it always distributes burdens to the disadvantage of the socially weak . . .
>
> It is our duty to play a leading role in such strikes and to link the purely economic demands with the political. National Socialism rejects strikes which are instigated for party-political reasons. . . .

Selected documents

Document 56
The NSBO attacks the official unions

The Socialist-inclined trade unions would be organising strikes within the capitalist order for the forseeable future. The NSBO denounced this approach as hopeless in the situation created by the Great Depression and suspected that union officials' self-interest determined their strategy.

From: 'Lohnabbau, Gewerkschaften und NSDAP', *Der Betriebs-Stürmer*, 2, 1931, p. 5.

> The attitude of the Trade Unions to wage cuts is generally known and holds few surprises. They resist them as best they can. 'As best they can' means they resist them badly. When they use economic arguments their case is so feeble that the employers have little trouble in refuting it. The Trade Unions know this, so they avoid this approach whenever possible. Instead they speak of the workers' desperate plight, but since the Trade Union officials themselves are usually motivated by completely different considerations, people notice the artificiality of their emotions all too easily. The main consideration of the Trade Unions is to save their own faces. They want to appear as the immovable unions, the ever-reliable guardians of the working-class cause – and want to retain the trust and the subscriptions of the workers.

Document 57
The NSBO condemns the Versailles Treaty and the ethos of capitalism

Versailles and capitalism were denounced here by the NSBO in anti-Semitic terms. They were regarded as a shabby betrayal of Germany, its workers, and its people in general by shady, often Jewish, international forces.

'Die Befreiung der deutschen Arbeit', *Der Betriebs-Stürmer*, 2, 1931, p. 2.

> The years 1914 to 1918 had nothing to do with the elimination of the princes and of militarism, as the Marxist Jewish press pretends. Instead they involved the destruction of the German Reich's economic pre-eminence and thus the freedom of German labour.
>
> November 1918 did not result in the deposition of the feudal lords to the benefit of the workers. Instead the 9 November brought the defeat of Germany as a state. But the German worker paid the price.

177

His masters today are the irresponsible, faceless, international big capitalists and the Jews of the banking world. If the worker was once his own master, free to work where he wanted and as it took him, he is now – in 'the freest republic on earth' – the coolie of international high finance, happy if he can work at all, whose one fear is to be sucked into the cogwheels of the welfare state with its benefit books and official stamps. If we once had four 'estates', the officially-recognised unemployed with their eligibility for benefits have now added a fifth.

National Socialism demands a transformation from the utterly unscrupulous profit-motivated economy to an economy geared to need. At the very least agriculture must be transformed to supply Germany's factory population with the necessary food and raw materials, and to adopt the opposite perspective, only a flourishing farming estate can serve as the best consumer of industrial and other products.

Document 58
The Communists blame the SPD for Nazi successes

In a curious way the Communists agreed with the Nazis about the Republic. The SPD had betrayed its natural supporters and the NSDAP had profited.

From: 'Eine rote Einheitsfront schlägt Hitler', *Die Rote Fahne*, 93, 30 April 1932.

Who are the new Nazi recruits? In part they are elements who were ready to participate in the Revolution of 9 November 1918 and then saw themselves sold down the river by the SPD leaders. A whole generation of adolescents were told: 'This is how the Marxists are ruining us!' and many of these young people confused the 'Marxism' of the SPD leaders with uncorrupted Marxism. Through their method of government the SPD leaders succeeded in discrediting Marxism among broad sections of the population.

Workers and the SA

Unlike the NSBO the SA was not and did not seek to be a labour organisation. Its ethos harked back to the 'Front Community' of the Great War which had purportedly transcended class interests. However, most of its recruits were young male workers who had lost their jobs during the Great Depression.

Document 59
A storm-trooper recounts his blighted career prospects

Joseph L. of Frankfurt-am-Main was a typical SA recruit. His curriculum vitae, written in 1933, relates the problems and disappointments of his working life.

From: Hessisches Hauptstaatsarchiv Wiesbaden, 483/2158, 81st SA Regiment, Frankfurt-am-Main.

As the son of the tramways worker Thomas L. I was born on 9 October 1904. I attended primary school from the age of six for eight years in Oberrad, Frankfurt. Upon leaving I trained as a toolmaker. After the completion of my three year apprenticeship I worked for a year in my trade, then I was made redundant because of a shortage of work. The prospects of getting another position in my trade were bad, so I sought work elsewhere. I found a job in a metal goods firm and worked there for three months as a storeman, then I was also made redundant here because of a lack of work. After three months without a job I got one as a packer and storeman in a metal goods firm. I worked seven years there until I was made redundant here too because of a lack of work. I have now been unemployed for two years and eight months.

Heil Hitler
Joseph L.

Document 60
A storm-trooper recalls his disillusionment with the SPD

Hermann T. of Frankfurt-am-Main was less typical in experiencing no personal difficulties in his working life. For him disillusionment with the SPD and a belief in Adolf Hitler's capacities as an emancipator were decisive in attracting him to the SA.

From: Hessisches Hauptstaatsarchiv Wiesbaden, 483/2277, 99th SA Regiment, Franfurt-am-Main.

On the 7 October 1909 I was born in Reiskirchen near Giessen as the son of the type-setter Michael T. I attended the Zentgrafen School in Frankfurt-am-Main/Seckbach from the age of six and graduated from the senior class there. I completed my three year apprenticeship as an electrical fitter at the firm of Karl Diehl. I was politically active in the Iron Front (SPD) for about one and a half years. After I had gradually become aware of the SPD's poor leadership and that its efforts couldn't help us, I resigned from the organisation. On the other hand, I am convinced that the new Germany, led by our People's Chancellor Adolf Hitler, signifies recovery and resurgence and I wish to devote all my efforts to this.

With loyal German Greetings
Heil Hitler
Hermann T.

Document 61
The KPD discusses the SA's membership

The Communists blamed the Socialists and capitalists for most of Weimar Germany's ills. However their discussion here of the SA members' motivation is much more perceptive and disturbing. From: Bundesarchiv R134/74, 127–8; National Ministry of the Interior, IAN 2166a of 23 December 1931.

National Fascism [the NSDAP] is the opposite side of the coin from Social Fascism [the SPD]. The betrayal of socialism, of the German working people and thereby of the German nation by the SPD's leaders has led millions of workers, rural workers and impoverished members of the middle classes into the ranks of the NSDAP. In particular the disciplined, militarily-trained storm sections of the NSDAP – the SS and SA – boast a high percentage of industrial workers and in particular unemployed proletarians. For sure the NSDAP, supported by finance capital, uses bribery to win over the unemployed masses. Unemployed who join the SA receive clothing and sometimes accommodation and board. But this bribery is not the decisive factor behind the flow even of the proletarian masses into the NSDAP. Decisive is the SPD's betrayal of socialism and the lying, pseudo-socialist demagogy of Hitler's party. We have to recognise that a large proportion of the Nazi proletarians are misled workers who honestly believe that they are fighting against capitalism and for socialism.

Works cited

Allen, William Sheridan, *The Nazi Seizure of Power. The Experience of a Single German Town 1930–1935*, London, 1966.

Berghahn, Volker, R., and Martin Kitchen (eds.), *Germany in the Age of Total War*, London, Totowa, NJ, 1981.

Bessel, Richard, *Political Violence and the Rise of Nazism. The Storm Troopers in Eastern Germany 1925–1934*, New Haven, London, 1984.

Bessel, Richard, 'The Rise of the NSDAP and the Myth of Nazi Propaganda', *Wiener Library Bulletin*, 33, 1980, pp. 20–9.

Bessel, Richard, and E. J. Feuchtwanger (eds.), *Social Change and Political Development in Weimar Germany*, London, Totowa, NJ, 1981.

Black, Antony (ed.), *Community in Historical Perspective. A translation of selections from Das deutsche Genossenschaftsrecht by Otto von Gierke*, trans. M. Fischer, Cambridge, New York, 1990.

Blackbourn, David, 'The Discreet Charm of the Bourgeoisie: Some Recent Works on German History', *European Studies Review*, 11, 1981, pp. 243–55.

Blackbourn, David, and Geoff Eley, *The Peculiarities of German History. Bourgeois Society and Politics in Nineteenth-Century Germany*, Oxford, New York, 1984.

Blackbourn, David, and Richard Evans (eds.), *The German Bourgeoise. Essays on the social history of the German middle classes from the late eighteenth to the early twentieth century*, London, New York, 1991.

Bracher, Karl Dietrich, *The German Dictatorship. The Origins, Structure and Effects of National Socialism*, trans. J. Steinberg, London, 1973.

Breuilly, John (ed.), *The State of Germany. The national idea in the making, unmaking and remaking of a modern nation state*, London, New York, 1992.

Brown, Jeremy R. S., 'The Berlin NSDAP in the Kampfzeit', *German History*, 7, 1989, pp. 241–47.

Works cited

Brozsat, Martin, *The Hitler State. The foundations and development of the internal structure of the Third Reich*, trans. J. W. Hiden, London, New York, 1981.

Buchloh, Ingrid, *Die nationalsozialistische Machtergreifung in Duisburg. Eine Fallstudie*, Duisburg, 1980.

Bullock, Alan, *Hitler and Stalin. Parallel Lives*, London, 1991.

Burleigh, Michael, and Wolfgang Wippermann, *The Racial State. Germany 1933–1945*, Cambridge, 1991.

Carsten, Francis, *The Rise of Fascism*, London, 1967.

Carsten, Francis, *Fascist Movements in Austria. From Schönerer to Hitler*, London, 1977.

Childers, Thomas, and Jane Caplan (eds.), *Reevaluating the Third Reich*, New York, London, 1993.

Degras, Jane (ed.), *The Communist International 1919–1943. Documents*, London, 1971.

Dusik, B. (ed.), *Hitler. Reden Schriften Anordnungen. Februar 1925 bis Januar 1933*, vol. 2(2), Munich, 1992.

Eley, Geoff, *Reshaping the German Right. Radical Nationalism and Political Change after Bismarck*, New Haven, London, 1980.

Eley, Geoff, *Fron Unification to Nazism. Reinterpreting the German Past*, Winchester, Mass., London, 1986.

Evans, Richard, and Dick Geary (eds.), *The German Unemployed. Experiences and Consequences of Mass Unemployment from the Weimar Republic to the Third Reich*, London, Sydney, 1987.

Falter, Jürgen W., *Hitlers Wähler*, Munich, 1991.

Fest, Joachim C., *The Face of the Third Reich*, trans. M. Bullock, London, 1972.

Feuchtwanger, E. J. (ed.), *Upheaval and Continuity. A Century of German History*, London, 1973.

Fischer, Conan (ed.), *Weimar, the Working Classes and the Rise of National Socialism*, Oxford, 1995, forthcoming.

Fischer, Fritz, *Germany's Aims in the First World War*, London, 1967.

Fischer, Fritz, *War of Illusions*, London, 1973.

Fischer, Fritz, *From Kaiserreich to Third Reich: Elements of Continuity in German History 1871–1945*, trans. R. Fletcher, London, Boston, Sydney, 1986.

Fletcher, Roger, *Revisionism and Empire: Socialist Imperialism in Germany 1897–1914*, London, 1984.

Fletcher, Roger, 'Revisionism and Wilhelmine Imperialism', *Journal of Contemporary History*, 23, 1988, pp. 347–66.

Fritzsche, Peter, *Rehearsals for Fascism. Populism and Political Mobilization in Weimar Germany*, New York, Oxford, 1990.

Geiger, Theodor, *Die Klassengesellschaft im Schmelztiegel*, Cologne, Hagen, 1949.

Works cited

Gorz, André, *Farewell to the Working Class. An essay on Post-Industrial Socialism*, trans. M. Sonenscher, London, 1982.

Guttsman, W. L., *Workers' Culture in Weimar Germany. Between Tradition and Commitment*, New York, Oxford, Munich, 1990.

Hamilton, Alastair, *The Appeal of Fascism. A Study of Intellectuals and Fascism 1919–1945*, New York, 1971.

Hamilton, Richard F., *Who Voted for Hitler?*, Princeton, NJ, 1982.

Hauner, Milan, 'Did Hitler Want a World Dominion?', *Journal of Contemporary History*, 13, 1978.

Heilbronner, Oded, 'Der verlassene Stammtisch. Vom Verfall der bürgerlichen Infrastruktur und dem Aufstieg der NSDAP am Beispiel der Region Schwarzwald', *Geschichte und Gesellschaft*, 19, 1993, pp. 178–201.

Hitler, Adolf, *Mein Kampf (My Struggle)*, London, 1938.

Kater, Michael J., *The Nazi Party. A Social Profile of Members and Leaders, 1919–1945*, London, 1983.

Kater, Michael J., *Doctors under Hitler*, Chapel Hill, London, 1989.

Kele, Max H., *Nazis and Workers. National Socialist Appeals to German Labor 1919–1933*, Chapel Hill, 1972.

Kershaw, Ian, *The Nazi Dictatorship. Problems and Perspectives of Interpretation*, London, 1985.

Kershaw, Ian, *Hitler*, London, New York, 1991.

Kitchen, Martin, *Fascism*, London, 1976.

Krabbe, Wolfgang R. (ed.), *Politische Jugend in der Weimarer Republik*, Dortmund, 1993.

Kubizek, August, *Young Hitler. The Story of our Friendship*, trans. E. V. Anderson, Maidstone, 1973.

Lane, Barbara Miller, and Leila J. Rupp (eds.), *Nazi Ideology before 1933. A Documentation*, Manchester, 1978.

Laqueur, Walter (ed.), *Fascism: A Reader's Guide: Analyses, Interpretations, Bibliography*, London, 1976.

Lipset, Seymour Martin, *Political Man. The Social Bases of Politics*, Baltimore, 1981.

McClelland, J. S. (ed.), *The French Right from de Maistre to Maurras*, London, 1970.

Mommsen, Hans, *Arbeiterbewegung und Nationale Frage. Aufgewählte Aufsätze*, Göttingen, 1979.

Mommsen, Hans, *Die verspielte Freiheit. Der Weg der Republik in den Untergang 1918 bis 1933*, Frankfurt-am-Main, Berlin, 1990.

Mühlberger, Detlef, *Hitler's Followers. Studies in the Sociology of the Nazi Movement*, London, New York, 1991.

Noakes, Jeremy, *The Nazi Party in Lower Saxony 1921–1933*, Oxford, 1971.

Nolte, Ernst, *The Three Faces of Fascism*, London, 1965.

Nolte, Ernst, *Der Europäische Bürgerkrieg: Nationalsozialismus und*

Bolschewismus, Berlin, 1987.

Parsons, Talcott, *Essays in Sociological Theory*, New York, 1949.

Peukert, Detlev, *The Weimar Republic: the crisis of classical modernity*, trans. R. Deveson, London, 1991.

Plamenatz, John, *Man and Society. Political and Social Theories from Machiavelli to Marx*, 2nd edn., London and New York, 1992.

Preller, Ludwig, *Sozialpolitik in der Weimarer Republik*, Düsseldorf, 1978.

Prinz, Michael, and Rainer Zitelmann (eds.), *Nationalsozialismus und Modernisierung*, Darmstadt, 1991.

Reichsorganisationsleiter der NSDAP (ed.), *Partei-Statistik. Stand 1. Januar 1935*, Munich, 1935.

Shirer, William L., *The Rise and Fall of the Third Reich*, New York, London, 1960.

Smelser, Ronald, and Rainer Zitelmann (eds.), *The Nazi Elite*, trans. M. Fischer, Basingstoke, London, 1993.

Stachura, Peter D., *Gregor Strasser and the Rise of Nazism*, London, Boston, Sydney, 1983.

Stachura, Peter D. (ed.), *The Nazi Machtergreifung*, London, Boston, Sydney, 1983.

Taylor, A. J. P., *The Course of German History. A Survey of the Development of Germany since 1815*, London, 1945.

Vermeil, Edmond, *Germany's Three Reichs. Their History and Culture*, trans. E. W. Dickes, London, 1945.

Wehler, Hans-Ulrich, *Sozialdemokratie und Nationalstaat. Nationalitäten-fragen in Deutschland 1840–1914*, Göttingen, 1971.

Weinberg, Gerhard (ed.), *Hitlers Zweites Buch. Ein Dokument aus dem Jahr 1928*, Stuttgart, 1961.

Winkler, Heinrich-August, *Mittelstand, Demokratie und National-sozialismus. Die politische Entwicklung von Handwerk und Kleinhandel in der Weimarer Republik*, Cologne, 1972.

Winkler, Heinrich-August, *Von der Revolution zur Stabilisierung. Arbeiter und Arbeiterbewegung in der Weimarer Republik 1918 bis 1924*, Berlin, Bonn, 1984.

Wiskemann, Elizabeth, *Czechs and Germans. A Study of the Struggle in the Historic Provinces of Bohemia and Moravia*, 2nd edn., London, New York, 1967.

Zeman, Z. A. B., *Nazi Propaganda*, 2nd edn., London, Oxford, New York, 1973.

Selected bibliography

The selection of a relatively small number of works on Nazism out of the thousands available can induce euphoria or despair: euphoria because of the numerous excellent works, despair because selection will, inevitably, be arbitrary to a degree. The following list will be confined to books published in English, although the reader will find a rewarding range of articles in the leading English-language journals. These include *German History, Central European History, The Journal of Contemporary History, European History Quarterly, Past and Present* and the *Journal of Modern History*.

Of general works Gordon A. Craig, *Germany 1866–1945*, Oxford, 1978, provides an outstanding introduction to the broader period. Specifically on Weimar, Eberhard Kolb, *The Weimar Republic*, London, 1988, includes a thorough narrative and analysis of historical debates, Peter Gay, *Weimar Culture*, London, 1969, is a classic in its field. The earlier sections of Karl Dietrich Bracher, *The German Dictatorship*, London, 1971, 1973, remain indispensable, if slightly dated, and are complemented by early chapters in Martin Broszat, *The Hitler State*, London, 1981, and his *Hitler and the Collapse of Weimar Germany*, Leamington Spa, 1987. A. J. Nicholls, *Weimar and the Rise of Hitler*, London, 1992, is a new edition of an established classic. Francis Carsten, *The Rise of Fascism*, London, 1967, includes detailed coverage of Germany. The most comprehensive documentary coverage of Nazism during Weimar is found in Jeremy Noakes and Geoffrey Pridham (eds.), *Nazism 1919–1945. A Documentary Reader*, Exeter, 1988. Edited volumes on the Weimar era include Richard Bessel and E. J. Feuchtwanger (eds.), *Social Change and Political Development in Weimar Germany*, London, Totowa, NJ, 1981; Peter D. Stachura (ed.), *The Shaping of the Nazi State*, London, 1978; Peter D. Stachura (ed.), *The Nazi Machtergreifung*, London, Boston, Sydney, 1983; Thomas Childers (ed.),

185

The Formation of the Nazi Constituency, 1919–1933, Totowa, NJ, 1986; and Ian Kershaw (ed.), *Weimar. Why did German Democracy Fail?*, London, 1990, which is especially useful on the economic history of the period. Looking specifically at the Great Depression and the collapse of Weimar, Richard Evans and Dick Geary (eds.), *The German Unemployed*, London, Sydney, 1987, and Peter D. Stachura (ed.), *Unemployment and the Great Depression in Weimar Germany*, London, 1986, include a range of valuable essays.

A large number of local/regional studies trace the rise of Nazism. Those in English include two classic works on Lower Saxony: William Sheridan Allen, *The Nazi Seizure of Power*, London, 1966 – on the town of Northeim – and Jeremy Noakes, *The Nazi Party in Lower Saxony*, Oxford, 1971. On other areas: Rudy Koshar, *Social Life, Local Politics and Nazism: Marburg 1880–1935*, Chapel Hill, NC, 1986, Geoffrey Pridham, *Hitler's Rise to Power. The Nazi Movement in Bavaria*, London, 1973.

On the historiography and ideology of Nazism: Walter Laqueur (ed.), *Fascism: A Reader's Guide: Analyses, Interpretations, Bibliography*, London, 1976, remains an excellent source on Nazism and fascism; Ian Kershaw, *The Nazi Dictatorship*, 3rd edn., London, 1993, includes a very useful introductory chapter; Martin Kitchen, *Fascism*, London, 1976, is succinct on the clasic theories; Andreas Dorpalen, *German History in Marxist Perspective*, London, 1985, presents and analyses East German, Marxist-Leninist interpretations; Barbara Miller Lane and Leila J. Rupp (eds.), *Nazi Ideology before 1933*, Manchester, 1978, contains key writings by Nazi leaders; Alastair Hamilton, *The Appeal of Fascism*, New York, 1971, includes a chapter on German intellectuals and Nazism. Ernst Nolte, *The Three Faces of Fascism*, London, 1965, is a classic, perhaps dated, exposition of the middle-class crisis in inter-war Europe; much more modern on Germany is Detlev Peukert, *The Weimar Republic: the crisis of classical modernity*, London, 1991. On Nazism's antecedents in the Austro-Hungarian Empire: Francis L. Carsten, *Fascist Movements in Austria: From Schönerer to Hitler*, London, 1977, and Elizabeth Wiskemann, *Czechs and Germans*, 2nd edn., London, New York, 1967.

On organisation Dietrich Orlow, *The History of the Nazi Party 1919–1933*, Pittsburgh, 1969, is thorough, Joseph Nyomarkay, *Charisma and Factionalism in the Nazi Party*, Minneapolis, 1967, Edward N. Peterson, *The Limits of Hitler's Power*, Princeton, NJ, 1969, and Jill Stephenson, *The Nazi Organisation of Women*, London, 1980, provide more specialised accounts. Peter D. Stachura, *Gregor Strasser and the Rise of Nazism*, London, Boston, Sydney, 1983, includes coverage of Strasser's career as Party Organiser. **Propaganda** is widely discussed: Z. A. B. Zemen, *Nazi*

Propaganda, London, Oxford, New York, 1973, contains a useful chapter on the pre-1933 period.

Turning to Hitler, Ian Kershaw, *Hitler*, London, New York, 1991, provides an authoritative introduction. Hitler himself should be read in D. C. Watt (intro), *Mein Kampf*, London, 1969, or Telford Taylor (intro), *Hitler's Secret Book*, New York, 1961. Eberhard Jäckel, *Hitler's Weltanschauung. A Blueprint for Power*, Middletown, Conn., 1972, examines Hitler's ideology. The classic English-language biography is Alan Bullock, *Hitler. A Study in Tyranny*, London, 1964; Alan Bullock, *Hitler and Stalin. Parallel Lives*, London, 1991, updates the author's assessment. Other important biographies include Joachim C. Fest, *Hitler*, London, 1974, and William Carr, *Hitler. A Study in Personality and Politics*, London, 1978. August Kubizek, *Young Hitler. The Story of our Friendship*, Maidstone, 1973, gives an account of Hitler's youth.

On the Nazi leadership, Joachim C. Fest, *The Face of the Third Reich*, London, 1972, is very readable; authoritative and more recent is Ronald Smelser and Rainer Zitelmann (eds.), *The Nazi Elite*, Basingstoke, London, 1993.

Political violence and paramilitary politics receive general treatment in J. M. Diehl, *Paramilitary Politics in Weimar Germany*, Bloomington, Ind. and London, 1977, on the Nazi movement generally Peter H. Merkl, *Political Violence under the Swastika. 581 early Nazis*, Princeton, NJ, 1975, explores the personal motivation of some veteran Nazis. On Communist/Nazi violence, E. Rosenhaft, *Beating the Fascists? The German Communists and Political Violence 1929–1933*, Cambridge, 1983, is very useful; on the SA, Richard Bessel, *Political Violence and the Rise of Nazism. The Storm Troopers in Eastern Germany 1925–1934*, New Haven, London, 1984, and Conan Fischer, *Stormtroopers. A Social, Economic and Ideological Analysis 1929–35*, London, 1983, place its history in the context of the radicalised lower middle class and unemployed working class respectively. Specifically on the 1923 *Putsch*, Harold J. Gordon, *Hitler and the Beer Hall Putsch*, Princeton, NJ, 1972.

The National Socialist electorate is investigated in two outstanding pioneering studies: Richard F. Hamilton, *Who Voted for Hitler?*, Princeton, NJ, 1982, and Thomas Childers, *The Nazi Voter*, Chapel Hill, NC, London, 1983. A translation is badly needed of Jürgen W. Falter, *Hitlers Wähler*, Münich, 1991, which is now the definitive work.

On party membership, Michael J. Kater, *The Nazi Party*, London, 1983, has been the standard source; his conclusions have been revised somewhat by Detlef Mühlberger, *Hitler's Followers*, London, New York, 1991, which also examines the SA and SS.

Establishment and middle-class support for Nazism is accorded valuable treatment in most of the authored and edited volumes cited above under general works. In addition there are two classic studies of the German military: Francis L. Carsten, *The Reichswehr and Politics 1918–1933*, Oxford, 1966, and relevant chapters in Gordon A. Craig, *The Politics of the Prussian Army, 1640–1945*, Oxford, 1975. Henry A. Turner, *German Big Business and the Rise of Hitler*, Oxford, 1985, and J. E. Farquharson, *The Plough and the Swastika. The NSDAP and agriculture in Germany, 1928–1945*, London, 1976, detail relations between two key economic sectors and Nazism. Middle-class populism is examined in Peter Fritzsche, *Rehearsals for Fascism*, New York, Oxford, 1990.

German labour and Nazism is less well covered. Max H. Kele, *Nazis and Workers. National Socialist Appeals to German Labor*, Chapel Hill, NC, 1972, was the most notable early work. Donna Harsch, *German Social Democracy and the Rise of Nazism*, Chapel Hill, NC, London, 1993, and Conan Fischer, *The German Communists and the Rise of Nazism*, Basingstoke, London, 1991, examine relations between the left-wing parties and the Nazis. Forthcoming is Conan Fischer (ed.), *Weimar, the Working Classes and the Rise of National Socialism*, Oxford, 1995.

Index

189

Index